Mariana S

On Angels' Wings

SoulLink Publisher

©2013 Mariana Stjerna and SoulLink Publisher
All Rights Reserved

ISBN 978-1484174647 (sc)
ISBN 978-91-978399-2-1 (pdf ebook)
Also available on Kindle

First printed in Swedish 1998

Support with translation and publishing: Aaron Rose, USA

Other books in English by Mariana Stjerna:
Agartha – The Earth's Inner World (2013)
The Bible Bluff (2013)
Mission Space (2013)

SoulLink Publisher
www.SoulLink.se
info@SoulLink.se

The Cosmic Map

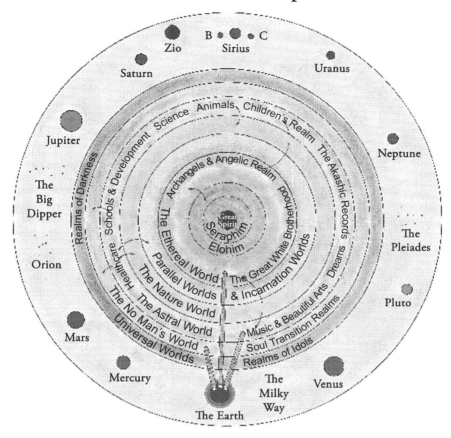

The Map rests on the starry sky. Here you can see the planets and some constellations in our galaxy. For a more detailed description, see page 195.

1 Universal Worlds
    1a Realms of Darkness
    1b Realms of Idols
2 The No Man's World
    2a Soul Transition Realms
3 The Astral World
    3a Realm of Healthcare
    3b Realm of Schools and Development
    3c Realm of Science
    3d Realm of Animals
    3e Children's Realm
    3f The Akashic Records
    3g Realms of Dreams
    3h Realms of Music and Beautiful Arts
4 The Nature World
5 Parallel Worlds and Incarnation Worlds
6 The Ethereal World
    6a Archangels and Angelic Realm
    6b Realm of the Masters (The Great White Brotherhood)
7 World of the Elohim
8 World of the Seraphim
(The Inner Core) The Great Spirit

Jan Fridegård (1897-1968) grew up as a farm laborer and tried several professions before the debut of his writings: *One Night in July* (1933). His autobiographical novel trilogy about Lars Hård is perhaps his finest work. The death of his father aroused a latent interest in the supernatural, which came to be reflected in *The Tower Rooster* (1941).

Contents

The Cosmic Map.. 3

Introduction.. 7

1. The Crossing 9
2. My Happy Valley 15
   The Akashic Records 17
3. Creation 23
   At First Came the Invisible Worlds.......................... 26
   The Fall of Lucifer 27
   Yin and Yang – Duality and Polarity......................... 28
   The First Humans – The People of the Sun and the Stars... 29
   Zio and the Migration to Earth 31
4. The Lost Millennium Kingdom................................. 35
   The Tale of Toja 39
5. The Nine Elders of Sirius 45
   The Reptile People... 47
6. In the Angels' School 55
   The Dual Flame... 57
7. The No Man's World 63
8. The Realms of the Astral World.............................. 71
   The Realms of Dreams 71
   The Realm of Music 78
   The Nature World 80
   The Realm of Animals 86
   The Children's Realm 89
9. The Midnight Mass 95
10. The Realm of Beautiful Arts 101
11. The Angelic Realm 105
    The Banquet... 109

About Soul Groups and Twin Souls.................................. 114

12. Meeting with the Master Djwal Khul 117
　　The Journey to Earth 118
　　How to Materialize and Dematerialize.......................... 123

13. Back to Shamballa.. 127
　　My Home Is in the Angelic Realm 130

14. Disobedience Is Punished 135

15. The Ashtar Command 141
　　Mission North America... 144
　　About Earthly Feelings and All-Love 148
　　My First Pupil 152

16. Helia and Sananda 157
　　The Goddess Helia: The Virgin Mary 157
　　An Opportunity to Ask Master Sananda Questions........ 161

17. Alien Contact... 167
　　A Political World Conference Gets a Cosmic Visit 170

18. About the Aura and the Chakras 175

19. About Prayer and Meditation 181
　　The Prayer of Mother Marta....................................... 182
　　The Creative Power of Thoughts................................. 187

20. Who Am I? An Existential Question 189
　　Appendix... 195
　　The Cosmic Map – Explanation and Guidance 195
　　The Original Meaning of Colors.................................. 198
　　List of Diseases and Colors... 199

Introduction

When I was asked to write this book I never hesitated. My Angelic companion Jan wanted to recount his personal experiences after death, from the moment of dying up to the present. He is a Spirit who, when he lived on Earth in the twentieth century, was a well-known writer in Sweden. He is a happy and humorous person, but also has profound experiences from the Cosmic Evolution. When he suggested that the name of the book would be *On Angels' Wings,* I at once associated this name with a memory from my childhood.

I love looking at the sky. Sometimes storm clouds gather in dark flocks, indigo-colored, with violet nuances. Sometimes there is a bright, blue sky strewn with fluffy, cotton wool puffs. When I was a young girl they were called "Angels' wings." I used to try to catch sight of a "real" Angel among them. Sometimes the dark clouds had gaps filled with light and I believed that within these was a sea of light where Angels flew, looking down at the silly humans through their cloud-windows. When they observed all the misery on Earth, they closed up the gaps with feathers from their wings.

When I asked Jan to tell me about Paradise he laughed heartily and answered, "What people think of as Paradise is not at all as they believe. Everyone creates his own Paradise – or whatever it is – with his own thoughts. I intend to start from the beginning, and the beginning for me is the end of my Earth life and the beginning of life before life."

"Are you in Paradise now?" I asked, somewhat naively.

"Oh no, I'm not!" he answered with a grin. "Your image of Paradise is not suitable for a rogue like me." He took a beautiful red autumn leaf and held it before my surprised eyes.

"This is but a small part of a living code," he went on. "It is a living code that can change its character, and yet it is a part of Eternity.

The leaf will fade, yet lives in full splendor and beauty, like mankind. Man has lost his closeness to Nature, and that is the key to his whole existence. If he loses that key he will also lose the meaning of his life. He will be trapped in his ego, which will take over his thoughts and actions. He will be the victim of misguided and impure energies. Please let me tell you a story that will be the greatest of all the stories you have heard."

Most people are not only scared of death, but also look on death as a punishment or something horrifying. I hope this book will remove such fears. No one can prove that my channeling from Jan is the Truth – but can you really talk about proof in this context? I am content to be the spokeswoman for a soul who has given me the information and inspiration to write *On Angels' Wings*. Now we will listen to a story told by Jan – a story that he, himself, will tell you from beginning to end.

– Mariana Stjerna

1. The Crossing

It has been a very long and hard step from the gray and poor farm laborer's cottage of my childhood to the well-established and wealthy author of today. When I grew older I was rather pleased with my life, especially when I jawed with colleagues and other such people. I was never afraid to tell the truth, but sometimes the truth was afraid of me. The ugly things in life have danced a waltz with the beautiful things, and that suited me. I constructed my books in the same way that you build a stone wall: big stones at the bottom and smaller ones on the top, with a little air in between. I have been a noisy person, arguing and nagging whenever I thought it necessary. I have always rubbed people the wrong way, and I continue to do so on the other side of the Light Portal.

If you think I exaggerate on occasions, please try to understand me. Up here I don't live on raw herring and potatoes. Our diet is different and I mostly try to be classy. This book will not deal with "small potatoes" (as we say in Sweden), but about something tremendous and somewhat inconceivable. It is unbelievable and magnificent! We are going to travel together in Worlds that have only one Law: the Cosmic Law, where Harmony meets Disharmony ending in both minor and major keys, making a chord of fantastic beauty.

I have described my life on Earth in books that are both autobiographical and educational. Now I am going to tell you about my *real* life, the life I was born into the moment I took my last breath on Earth. I now understand that the poor life in a farm laborer's cottage wasn't as trying and laborious as I thought it was at that time. I was at one with Nature, as I, day by day, in sunshine and rain, tended my cattle and repaired fences or worked hard with the soil. I learned to understand all the signs of Nature which were given to me in abundance.

My open mind received new impressions and secrets from season to season, but at that time I didn't understand how valuable the school of Nature was.

Mine was the sky – cloudy, clear, or gray and rainy. Mine was the ground with its riches, even when the snow covered the sleeping plants, their struggle for birth and rebirth in the new Spring, in the new, clear light. Mine was the marshy ground that watered my dirty, tired feet – friendly in summertime and deceitful in other seasons. The trees were telling me of their fear of being slaughtered by men craving money – and of their happiness, being able to stretch their crowns towards heaven. Bushes and weeds told another story of a stinging world, full of hideaways for all sorts of creepy-crawlies. I did not understand then what a wonderful place life was!

Much later I became friends with the poor farm boy in me and defended his right to be human in a society where people were treated far from equal. I learned to accept but also to question and not to swallow whole everything I was told. There are always flowers in summertime. They wink and flirt from the verges, because they know their place. The road must be free of flowers. On the road, traffic rushes by without seeing them. They exist, but they must not disturb the cold, gray stretch of asphalt. It is the same in life: There are flowers at the side of the road. Do you really have time to stop and pick some of them, without disturbing the entirety of the landscape? I think that you should. You have to pick them, or life will be transformed into an eternal freeway with no dreams and no beauty.

Now we will talk about my Birth into a completely different life. I closed my eyes in my Earth-life and stepped straight into the next life. I will tell you about the new life that started at the same time as my last breath!

How strange! I was breathing and felt bright and breezy! I looked at myself lying lifeless in my bed, but I didn't like what I saw. 'The old man has really aged,' I thought, 'and is as ugly as sin! Once I was a handsome man … No, I was not, I am!'

Where did this knowledge come from, that I am what I am – Now?

I turned my eyes from the old man in the bed and discovered a shiny, silvery, and very thin thread or ray between him and me. 'Exactly like a dog's leash,' I thought, and I laughed out loud. But the man at the other end of the leash didn't laugh. He looked dead. Suddenly I understood that that was precisely what he was: dead. I thought, 'Then who am I? I was him, and now I am him too!'

Sometimes you read about things like that. I was Jan's spirit now! I didn't feel any different – but I was very curious. Jan was dead – long live Jan!

The dog's leash was there the whole time. It is normally called the silver cord. I knew very well that I had to endure it for about three days. After that it would loosen by itself, like the umbilical cord of a newborn baby. In fact, I had read a lot about what happens after death. But now, when I was really there, in the middle of the Unknown, I felt uncertain. What does a human being really know about what happens after death, about life between lives? There are many theories – I always had a lot of them. But now … Where was I going? Where was the borderline between theory and knowledge?

People came into the room where the dead Jan lay – the dead Jan who was really alive! I recoiled and discovered that the silver cord could be stretched. I went out through the wall and I thought – sarcastic as I was – about my book called *The Tower Rooster*. Would I do the same thing as the old man in the book – hang on the outside of the tower – or would I get a lot further? In that case, how?

A pair of hands clutched mine. I was lifted through walls and the roof and I caught a glimpse of a huge entity dressed in white. The entity pulled me with him/her, gently but resolutely. The "dog-leash" was still there, but I didn't care, it must stretch a long way. We flew through the air like in some science-fiction novel. 'Maybe,' I thought, 'maybe they are telling the truth!' I laughed, because I used to write very down-to-earth prose. I saw no church towers, I didn't see the landscape the way you see it from an airplane. Maybe we flew through clouds, maybe it was some other fog, but I saw nothing. It grew dark now and it felt as if we were going through a tunnel. I closed my eyes. The unknown hands still grasped mine very firmly. It was strange how nice and safe it felt.

I couldn't resist pondering over what was going to happen to the other Jan, the one down on Earth. Was he to be buried in the cold soil or be eaten by fire? Maybe it was good not to know. I decided to leave it to this other person, who I presumed was an Angel. Well, if I hadn't gone astray or down the wrong track, of course! (But we seemed to go upwards, not downwards!)

I couldn't help smiling at that black thought, and at that moment we landed. I opened my eyes. I must admit I feared being surrounded by a burning Gehenna. Instead there was a large plain. I saw shapes rushing by – thin, transparent, foggy shapes.

'Oh,' I thought, and sighed gloomily, 'First you get to a kind of preliminary stage of purgatory. I know my Bible. After that it's all downhill. Well, I deserve it!'

"Am I like those?" I asked, and pointed at some ghost-like shapes gliding by.

"Not at all!" answered my winged companion with a smile. "You're like me!"

I looked more closely at her. She was dressed in a long, pale garment. She had blonde hair which reached her waist, and her large dark-blue eyes had the color of a summer-night's sky. She was not as tall as I had first imagined. Or perhaps she had shrunk after our swift journey? She was not transparent, but she seemed very light and lithe. Then I looked at my hands. They were still my hands, but they were softer and smoother.

"I am called Jolith and I am your Guardian Angel," she continued. "Jan, your physical body is dead, but you are alive! As long as the silver cord still remains between you and your body on Earth, your eyes will be veiled. When it is broken we will see where your free will leads you. I will remain with you for a time, but the day will come when you won't need me anymore."

"Why? Where are you going?" I asked. I was curious to know everything about my new friend. We had only just met; why was she talking of leaving?

"I will have a new mission," she answered in an evasive way. She still held my hand. She had a strong grip, as my father used to say. He judged people by their handshake and he didn't like what he called a woman's handshake. "They feel like dead herrings," was his rather harsh judgment. I suddenly longed very much for him. Why was he not here to meet me, in order to show me around heaven, laughing in his noisy way? If this was heaven, of course. I doubted it; everything was too simple and too foggy. I was not yet sure. Perhaps I had ended up in purgatory. A priest would have known; priests have a knack for that. Perhaps the vicar at home was now preaching about purgatory at my funeral. I wouldn't be surprised. I have said many bad things about priests.

"This is only the beginning, Jan, and not what you think." The Angel-girl smiled. "You will feel different when the cord has gone. Part of you is still on Earth. This is not what you would call Heaven."

"Is there really a Heaven?" I mockingly asked.

"There are many!" Jolith answered, and her sea-blue eyes glittered. "Wait and see!"

I yielded. I had always been curious about what happens after death, and here I was, holding hands with a beautiful girl, while faceless shadows were passing like a shoal of eels, clearly without a goal in this colorless existence. "Am I forced to live here with these shadows? Who are they?" I allowed myself to ask. I looked at her. She was as pretty as a picture – her blond hair and rosy cheeks could have been painted by Botticelli. Was I dreaming? Was I really dead? Was this really purgatory?

"No, my dear," she answered, although I never voiced the question. "You can see the shadows who have not liberated themselves from their Earthly bonds, although their silver cords were loosened long ago. They are Earth-bound souls who are mourning their life on Earth. Some of them are disappointed, some are discontented, and some are confused. Some of them are even chained to their own sins and misfortunes. They refuse to go further."

"I want to go further, my beautiful Beatrice!" I jested, and my lovely companion smiled warmly. We exchanged a look of mutual understanding. Suddenly Jolith pricked up her ears. She grabbed my arm and pulled me away from where we were standing. The fog grew dense and rolled itself around us like a thick, gray spiral.

"You are free from the silver cord! We can go on now!" exclaimed the Angel.

"Well, that was quick!" I pointed out, "Those were three fast days and nights!" I had learned that the cord is broken after three days and nights. How could this be?

"Time doesn't exist here," Jolith objected. "On the other hand, three days and three nights passed on Earth. Do you understand? I have been given the signal to proceed. The poor shadows here do not want to listen to their Guardian Angels. They prefer to wander about, homeless, as vague shapes until they understand that they have free choice to evolve in a new world. Sometimes their longing takes them back to Earth. They cannot stay there, but they willingly wander about the outskirts of their old life perpetually."

"Is that what we call ghosts?" I asked.

"Yes, they are the visible invisible people," was the answer. "It is possible for them to influence people in the places they choose to appear, in dreams and suchlike. Sometimes love for their old environment gives them a positive force, but mostly this force is negative and limited because of the fear they meet there. Most living people are afraid of ghosts, you see. But now, Jan, let us proceed, if you don't want to stay here among the shadows."

Of course, I didn't want to stay. Nevertheless it might have been fun to haunt some friends, my publisher for instance, and some other old friends. I could imagine them at my graveside, hats in hand. They were probably drinking a couple of schnapps at the funeral feast in my honor. But of course I was very curious to find out what was waiting "upstairs" or "further on" – whichever it was.

Jolith started to grow in the cloudy spiral. She took me in her arms and I rested there as on an eiderdown comforter. At the same time I felt as if I were in a mother's womb – with labor pains. I was infinitely small and also very curious about the world outside. Then all became dark for a moment – or for an eternity. Is there any difference here, in this beingness?

2. My Happy Valley

Life was smiling at me when I awoke. What else other than life could guide me to such a lovely and idyllic spot? I wished I could laugh and dance around with my beautiful Angel, who again was small and dainty. She smiled and said, "Do it, Jan! Dance with me!"

We danced on a sunny flowerbed, where scent and music was one, where the air vibrated with sounds, enclosing us in a breathless embrace. We were as light as air itself, yet I felt my feet touching the dewy grass that was glittering below me. I felt my right arm around the Angel's thin waist and my left hand held hers in a close grip that seemed almost physical. It was such a long time since I had been able to dance, and I enjoyed the lovely music from the invisible musicians and the pleasure of the boisterous dance.

"Now we must proceed," Jolith commanded. "We just danced in the valley where your last life started. Look around you!"

I had totally forgotten to look where I was. I was entirely intoxicated by the dance, the music, and the fragrances, but now I could see high mountains close around us. They were moss-covered, and trees blossomed in splendid colors everywhere. The mountaintops were bare, but they were shining in a magical way. It was as if the mountains had halos. 'The mountains of the saints,' I thought with a smile. I saw a river that murmured and babbled in capricious curves, until it tumbled happily over a steep cliff-edge and became a magnificent waterfall. The plant life around it was highly colored and fresh. It was a sublime Earthly landscape.

"From here you decided to return to Earth and live your last life there," said the Angel. "Between lives you were here, because you are a part of this valley. You are the grass, the flowers, and the trees. You are the silent, vigilant mountains and the water that runs in sweet streams until it throws itself into the creation of your next life. You always loved this place. Don't you remember it?"

"Yes," I answered, and I was amazed. "The memory of it is coming back to me! This is my happy valley where I can find my origin. How could I ever leave this paradise to go to hell on Earth?"

"You had to," sighed my Guardian Angel. "You chose it in order to get exactly the experiences you gained on Earth. It was in fact on that condition that you will walk your future path."

"Walk? Can I no longer decide for myself? I want to stay here. Who has the right to determine my path?"

"A long time ago you yourself chose to return to your origin and gather your experiences from many lives and many worlds. Your Inner Self makes your decisions, but the Great Spirit is guiding you. When we danced together it was the happy ratification of your new walk of life. Just feel how life is flowing inside you!"

"The dance of circulation." I laughed, and rotated another turn with the pretty girl. "Are we going to stay here or do we go on?"

"We stayed here for a moment of eternity," she answered. "Now you will meet one of the Counselors who will keep you company for a very long time."

She floated towards one of the high mountains. I followed her – perhaps a little reluctantly. The more I saw and heard, the more I wanted to know about this place. Why such a hurry? I wanted to know about my last stay here. How did I look? How did I think? Did I really choose to go back to Earth to be a poor farm boy in a tied cottage? Okay, perhaps it was good for me not to be born to a snob. I wonder how I would have coped with that? I laughed at the idea of me as a snob, and turned around to look at the adorable landscape.

Then I heard a man's voice talking to me, "Well, Jan, you became a cultural snob anyway!" Again I turned around in surprise. There was a tall man in a yellow cloak in front of me. His hair was snow-white but his face was young. He had a sharp profile. His features seemed to be chiseled by a Greek artist and his deep-blue eyes were full of life. He looked inquiringly at me with a nice, friendly smile.

I instinctively felt that he was a humorous man.

"It's time for you to be confronted with yourself," he continued. "What you have been and what you are will together form what you become."

"Oh yes!" I exclaimed, "the Akashic Records! This is where all one's mistakes and silly ventures are revealed, isn't it? May I ask who you are?"

"My name is Zar," he answered, and his eyes glittered. "Silly things are not the only things you did, my friend. I will be your leader and teacher as long as you need me. The Akashic Records" (see the Cosmic Map on page 3) "is a kind of intermediate stage between two worlds. Everybody must experience it. Afterwards it is decided which world you belong to – so please, let's get it done!"

The walls of the mountain we had reached rose almost perpendicularly up to the sky – whatever sky it might be, I thought. I still remember the lovely sunset over the mountains and the forest of my childhood. This was yet more beautiful. The sky above the mountain turned red and then became the most marvelous rose color, with golden hues. The man at my side touched the mountain with a staff. The mountain wall started to shake, and raised itself like a theatre curtain. There was a room behind it, furnished with comfortable chairs. In front of them was an enormous movie screen, which went from wall to wall. The room was dimly lit. We sat down, all three of us, with me in the middle. Between the screen and us was a little podium with a lighted floor. Sweet music came from somewhere.

The Akashic Records

"Are you ready?" asked Zar. "Be prepared for meetings of both good and bad. The principal figure here is Truth – the Truth that has followed you through thousands of years."

"The Truth about the country bumpkin Jan," I laughed. "Come along, I know for sure what a rogue and rascal I have been."

Zar looked at me in a strange way. "Well, we know that you liked that rogue and rascal," he said. "To love oneself is very important for a creative person. You became a beloved author, and do you know why? Soon we will learn if Jan the human is a reflection of the author Jan – or the opposite. We will know what you repent of and what you will forgive in yourself."

I was just about to give him a sharp retort of what I most repented of, when suddenly the movie screen darkened. There was lightning and thunder, and it rained in the room inside the mountain, but we remained dry. We were sitting dry-shod in a terrible storm. Flashes lit the moist mountain walls, and their granular surface looked as if it was sprinkled with diamonds.

"Raise your consciousness!" Zar ordered, and put his hand over mine.

Suddenly I felt how my Earthly thoughts disappeared and my whole inner Self experienced a euphoric feeling of light and radiant colors. Tears of happiness rolled down my cheeks. The storm and rain ceased and I saw the woods and meadows of my childhood on the screen. I saw my own birth and my father standing at my mother's side. He was chewing his mustache because he was both proud and terrified. He was proud to have another son, but afraid that my mother would be weakened. It all went well. I saw myself grow up, my life as a man with my own family – wife, son, and daughter. I cried, feeling ashamed and happy and also proud of all the good things life had given me. I was appalled at the dark sides and happy to have passed them in a tolerable way.

"What a life!" I exclaimed between laughter and weeping. "Is it possible to forgive such folly? Can you forget such injuries? Can you proceed, borne down by such a burden?"

"You have a strong back, Jan!" answered Zar. "Now take your chance to say hello to your parents, because the meeting will be very short."

There they were: my father and mother and my beloved little sister. They were as transparent as I was, but when we hugged each other their bodies seemed warm and substantial.

I thought we were talking the way we used to. Suddenly I

understood something. Nobody was moving their mouths – neither Zar, the Angel, father, mother, nor my darling sister. Was I? I was talking eagerly and put my finger against my lips. My lips weren't moving. This was a shock! When I looked at their faces I suddenly realized they had discovered the same strange thing. At first I felt like a ventriloquist, but when my father laughed his boisterous laugh noiselessly, I understood that this new body didn't work like the old, worn-out one.

I was still thinking about this when my relatives disappeared. Other faces, from my last life on Earth, showed themselves to me from the podium. Some of them were more well-known than others, as they appeared before me. Some of them screamed angrily at me and I was happy that they couldn't move their mouths. Wrongs and injustices, battles and insolence passed by. Dear old friends came forward to shake hands. It all ended with the darkening of the movie screen.

"Now we will return to your former incarnations!" It was Zar talking. "What fun to see if you have developed over those thousands of years." Now began a terrible and thrilling story.

I was a monk in the fourteenth century and a nobleman with a powdered wig in a Swedish castle in the eighteenth century. I had been a fisherman in Greece, where I met Death in an angry sea. I had been a Roman nobleman in the time of Jesus and also a poor soldier in Finland. Each life that was shown to me brought back my memory. I felt characterized by every one of these lives, but underneath the expressions of all of these lives I knew that I was me. The changes were superficial, but the inner Johan Fridolf Johansson From, alias Jan Fridegård, remained the whole time under the surface, seeking and groping, longing for something and full of a passion for justice. If I was a hunter, I was hunting injustice and duplicity. If I was a nobleman, I hunted ladies. All the time Jan was there, but I had a thousand faces.

I sailed on the sea of life and I had never suspected how thrilling it would be. My subconscious mind brought images of sweat and tears, but also of strength and courage in my last life on Earth. I decided to stay where I was. I had done my share on Earth. I had seen everything, experienced everything. If I chose to return to Earth, my life would only be a repetition – a bloated duck on a melancholy lake. Oh no, up here it was much more exciting.

"You want to stay here, Jan? And not go back to your dark green woods and your life as an author in the big, bright city?" Zar looked at me in an amusing way and added, "Look here! This is a picture of Stockholm today. Imagine how it would be to live there!"

I looked in tense expectation and hoped that my favorite restaurants would appear. Perhaps I might happily stroll through the Old Town. I would have welcomed any images of my lovely, old city. But what did I see? I was frightened and disappointed, and I literally felt my hair stand on end.

Chaos! Violence, stress, the rushing about, rough-mannered fellows, and even young girls who snatched handbags from old ladies and kicked them. I saw children hit children, children who were not children any longer. I saw pictures of drugs, alcohol, assaults, cruelty. Covetous, greedy-for-power people. Strange strangers, alienation – a city that was far removed from my memory of the old, friendly, and warm atmosphere. Trouble everywhere. I hid my face in my hands. I didn't want to see any more. I never again wanted to return to that.

"Don't criticize!" Zar warned. "The cities are what time has made them. Nobody will force you to enter that future. You still have your free will."

I don't know how long I remained in the mountain room with the big screen and holograms. Whatever I saw happened in a three-dimensional reality mixed with unreality. Time doesn't exist here, and when we were finished we left as easily as if this performance had only lasted an hour. Zar asked me if I repented of anything from my lives.

"How could I?" I answered. "It was all a question of development. I learned something all the time. Yet I didn't learn everything and I want to know more!"

"That's a good answer," my teacher said with a warm smile. "Now you can proceed if you like."

"Does every person who dies come here and look at his or her Akashic Record?" I asked.

"Of course," Zar answered. "We have this kind of review-room in many places. Some people are really shocked, because their memories return with every life they look at. It can be difficult for them to relive old unprocessed experiences. You did well because you understand yourself, just as you have analyzed Jan in every book you have written. There are many roads to walk after the Record. If you want to go further, please follow me."

3. Creation

With a sigh of relief I left the mountain room with Zar. We walked along a long, illuminated passage. I don't know how long we walked side by side, talking about interesting things, but suddenly the passage ended. We entered into a light that blinded us, and at first I couldn't see anything. I shaded my eyes with my arm and discovered a person right in front of us. It was impossible to see if it was a man or a woman, but the being was radiant. I fell on my knees, I felt such veneration. Maybe it was an Archangel?

The being lifted me up in a friendly way and I guessed it was a woman. She had long light-red hair, very dark eyes, and expressed warmth and friendliness.

"Welcome to us, Jan!" she smiled. "I am not an Archangel but I am an Angel, and your teacher. My name is Shala, and Zar and I will teach you the ancient wisdom and show you who you are and where you have come from. On Earth your thirst for knowledge was already great, and it brought you to us and to the Angels' School."

This lovely creature was thus a woman, and also my teacher. I longed for these lessons. But where was the school?

"Here!" answered Zar, who obviously read my thoughts. He made a circular gesture. "You have just passed a tunnel that leads to the Angelic Realm. From here you are going to experience your origin."

The blinding light had faded and I looked around. Again I was in a kind of theatre with three walls. The fourth wall was open and I caught a glimpse of a beautiful garden outside. Pictures started to appear on the empty walls. Human images floated in and out of the walls. These images showed people dressed in very old-fashioned clothes and they reminded me of Native Americans. At first I thought the whole scene was a confused fluttering of beings with and without faces. Yet I observed a certain rhythm. Suddenly it all became dark.

"You saw the first humans on their way to Earth," Shala explained. "The original inhabitants came from another planet. The knowledge they taught is still kept in secret custody inside Earth, but so far it has been too early to unveil it to humanity. At the beginning of the twenty-first century Truth will be necessary for people, and someone or something has to tell them about it before the whole Earth explodes because of human imprudence."

"I can imagine that." I felt very gloomy at the thought. "When I died at the end of the 1960s the pollution had already begun. Both the inner and the outer pollution. Can you do something about it? Do you want the destruction of Earth?"

"Of course not," the confident voice of Zar answered. "We work under high pressure to inform humanity of this, and many people have really started to listen. You belong to the ones who will be taught to have contact with an Earth-dweller who can send this message forward. You will have a lot to learn for this mission, and must go through tests and initiations."

"I don't know if I'm good enough for that," I muttered. "Me having contact with someone on Earth? I would like to be spared that!"

"You are going to inspire a woman on Earth, and with her medial mind and yours, she will be able to write books about the eternal Truth," explained Shala.

"Oh dear, do I have a good publisher waiting for me, too?" I joked.

"We will try to arrange that." Zar smiled. "So, my dear Jan, you will remain an author even here. Would you like that?"

"It's okay," I said mockingly. "If the lady in question is quick on the uptake, if she can behave and appreciate my advice, she will do. But tell me, will I see more of the first people on Earth?"

"In time," Zar answered. "But first you will experience something else. You, yourself, will take part at the birth of Earth! You are as old as we are – billions of years. Let our consciousness be born together on a journey on Angels' wings. Let our souls wake up in the sea of Eternity, at the feet of the Great Spirit you call God. You will experience what few human souls have ever seen. Jolith will take us to the goal on her great wings. She has the gift to appear in many forms, and we call upon her – Now!"

Sometimes I have silly thoughts, but I couldn't resist thinking that this was much better than the spiritual seances I attended on Earth. I had scarcely finished thinking this when my Guardian Angel appeared, in a giant woman's body. She lifted me and rolled me in one of her wings. Both my teachers were already on the other wing. I had another macabre thought: the dead man having an adventure, when we swept right through the wall and into a kind of pulsating corridor. Where were we going?

The answer came more swiftly than expected. A door in the corridor opened and Jolith flew out … out into the cosmos. Everything was air, a midnight-blue, clear, and lovely air. There was no light, not the slightest ray of light, yet I could see and feel. I was sitting on a soft white feather of Jolith's wing and suddenly the wing unfolded and Shala crept up to me, holding a mirror before my eyes. I saw absolutely nothing in that mirror. At first I was terrified. Don't I have a face any longer? I was just going to ask that when I recalled the handsome young soldier Jan who flirted with the girls on the open-air dance floor. Again it was a silly thought and it vanished.

Then I heard a voice whisper in my ear, "Jan, you are a grain of dust in our Universe! A grain of dust has no thoughts, but you will have the privilege to understand and remember what your teachers tell you. Now look around in your new consciousness!"

Someone pushed me, and I slid down the wing as if on some chute. I blew around in a whirling reality that was the cosmos, like the evening sky seen from our porch at home on a night without moon and stars. Of course I didn't think that, because I was only a newborn consciousness in a grain of dust on a dark blue night, without planets or stars. But the Power of Love was in the making, and there were other Universes, already finished. The grain of dust that I was knew nothing of this, but the dancing wind brought voices that sang the song of Creation, which I couldn't hear or understand.

Then the Light came, and in it the Power of Love. The Eternal Spirit that rules our Universe had divided its power, so that it flowed through the indigo-colored darkness. I was pulled into the Light and grew inside this living, creative, inspiring glare to an Energy, a ray with a glimpse of a greater consciousness. And yet I was still a very young Energy.

The radiating Power of Love had come to stay in our Universe. A small breath from its glowing center was transformed to a tone – and Sound was born. The Power of Love divided itself and became dual, male and female, yin and yang. Small Particles were thrown out of the Light into space, with magnificent swiftness and strength. Throughout eons of different kinds of development, they eventually formed stars and planets in our galaxy.

At First Came the Invisible Worlds

The loving breath from this magnificent Spirit started the Creation. At first the Invisible Worlds were created. The visible, physical celestial bodies are all very young. I was even younger than them when I took a rest in my own energy stream while the Highest Consciousness was involved in the process of creation. I was still in this light when a strange spectacle unfolded itself in my dreaming consciousness.

The Invisible Worlds were populated first. I was an energy-form that observed this unique act of creation. The dual characters of the Divine Spirit were shown as vague contours in the light. I was also an energy-form and because of that, I could approach them. Then I perceived a thought that permeated their radiance. It was a beautiful thought that expressed a longing to populate the innermost light-world with the same wonderful beauty that the Greatest Spirit himself had brought to his Universe. This divine beauty was to be reflected in all that was created!

At first the Seraphim were created in the innermost vicinity of the Divine. (See the Cosmic Map!) The tone that sounded in the cosmos formed the most lovely creatures with its resonance. These creatures became the servants of music, those who rule the world of tones. It was a form of mutual beingness, an origin of sound that eventually created the music of the spheres. The Seraphim were slender and transparent. Their fair hair floated around as a glittering light in an air that had not yet any sun, wind, or rain. They were the souls of a sacred music, and their whole existence was all about expressing the countless faces of Love in tones.

After that I saw the Angelic Realm grow before my startled "eyes" that were not yet eyes, just feelings. Now I wanted to be born, and I tried to tell that to the Wholeness by shaking and fidgeting. I was weary fluttering about on energy-waves without a body, without being able to communicate. I longed to be created – but it wasn't yet time for the energy-waves.

The Angels were divided in different Realms. There were seven Elohim and seven Archangels. To begin with, the Elohim were chosen to rule over all the planets and stars in the galaxy. The Archangels represented law and order in the Angelic Realm. There are thousands of different kinds of Angels, and they must be strictly organized. The Cherubim were the lightweights of Joy. They were – and are – messengers between the stars. I saw them emerge and develop into small rosy and joyful beings, always willing to share their positive gifts with others. I remained for a long time in the light of the Angelic paradise and I didn't know what I wanted, because I had no unique soul. I was just a part of the Oneness of Light.

The Fall of Lucifer

There was a disturbance in all this light energy. I felt it as a cold draught in the middle of my love-energy. My teachers talked to me with voices that were thoughts that were perceived, apprehended in the sea of light. We existed in an eternal beingness until the winds of change came riding, when the centuries became centuries and the moment for the birth of physical creation was near. Something happened among the Angels.

One of the Archangels was called the Light-carrier, or Lucifer. He became angry, because he thought his power was too limited. He made heavy demands, which were refused, because otherwise order could be disturbed. Angrily he left his position as an Archangel and created his own kingdom. Many Angels followed him, because he was loved by them. They imagined he was expelled from the Heavenly Realms, but his Father and his brothers could not understand why he left them so suddenly. Nobody decided anything without consulting the Father. Why was he not satisfied with his mission to bring the Light further, to care for it and develop it?

In the beginning Lucifer was not evil, just haughty. He never planned to leave his Father's house for good. His brothers were prepared to hug him lovingly when he came back. But neither he nor any of the Angels that followed him ever returned. In Lucifer's new kingdom there was a kind of eclipse, and out of it came evil. Gradually creatures were created that should never have been allowed to exist, and Lucifer gave them a leader. In the beginning it was only a defiant game, but the leader was evil because Lucifer had lost his gift to create with Love. There was no Love in his kingdom.

The leader had horns like a goat, and he was called the devil, or the evil one. He grew in power and strength and soon took power from Lucifer. He imprisoned the lost Angel and put him in a far-away tower. Lucifer would have stayed there for eternity, if he had not deeply repented his sin. After thousands of years he was brought back to the Angels of Light. He was forgiven and he now belongs to the team that will rescue Earth. He knows the ways of Evil and that is why he is the best one to oppose it.

Yin and Yang – Duality and Polarity

Behind the floating energy of Light I – Jan – had a soul that experienced all this as a repetition of life. I could put questions to my two teachers, and I did. I could hear them and sense their nearness, but not yet see them. I asked how the Angels were created from the beginning, whether they had different sexes, and how they multiplied.

Shala answered me with a sweet laugh. "You have experienced the first tone and sound. At that time there was already movement in the Universe, and in this movement we existed as more and more conscious energies. From some of these energy rays or energy-points, the Great Spirit created the Angels. I don't know exactly how. He brought with him, from his own origin, the ability to create. Before human beings were created, the Angels were just Angels. Later they were divided into many different groups. Right from the beginning there were male and female Angels, but also hermaphrodite entities.

"There are always two poles, yin and yang, because the Great Spirit is also dual. Duality and polarity are Laws in our cosmos. Love between all His creations is so strong that it unites them all and they don't multiply the way humans do, with a sexual act. The creation of Angels is a process more beautiful than you can ever imagine. During song, music, and marvelous performances of color, the duals are united in a way that forms a new Angelic Being.

"Angels have gifts of all kinds, like humans. They are given their missions according to their special talents. They have built the Angelic Realm by themselves from the beginning. You will be surprised when you see it, because of its resemblance to Earth. Landscapes and buildings are similar, but in more beautiful colors and lighter materials."

The First Humans –
The People of the Sun and the Stars

"Tell me, how was man created?" was my next question. "The Bible says that Adam was the first human and Eve was created from his ribs. Is that right?"

"There is no similarity whatsoever between what your Bible says and the original, ancient Truth," answered the voice of Zar. "You will experience the Truth in time, you little energy-beam in the great Light! We are with you now, as we always have been."

Suddenly I felt myself pulled out of the light, where I had been floating for such a long time. I was led into another, softer light. A huge Being, magnificent and inexpressibly beautiful, was talking, and the words were echoing in me like a booming trombone. I felt veneration on the verge of sacred worship. I just wanted to float into this tremendous Being of Love.

"I created the Angels in beauty and harmony," explained the Divine One. "That is why they are so fair. Because I love them deeply and they are images of my power, I want to create the inhabitants of the planets in their likeness. There are already planets inhabited by creatures that have just developed. They have no souls but are very technically gifted. Now I want to create a dwelling for the soul that is worth all the love, beauty, and joy it contains, and therefore I say, 'Let There Be Man!'"

The gigantic collection of energies which, like magnets, had been pulled into the enormous, radiating character of the Creator, all shivered when a wonderful tone accompanied his words and burst into giant fireworks. These fireworks were firing in the middle of the strong cosmic light. From this sparkling, flashing, fantastic Light, characters came swimming, soaring, and gliding. At first I felt like a spectator, but then, suddenly, I felt myself growing.

I looked down at my body. I had a body! It wasn't yet distinct and dense, but it had a head, arms, and legs like all the other entities around me. We were surrounded by lovely Angels who were singing and dancing and enfolding us with their wings. Next to me both my teachers floated. They were also a little diffuse, but easy to recognize. They took my hands, and in the twinkling of an eye, in a fraction of a second, we were transferred from the sunny energies of this indeterminable existence to solid earth made of clay and soil, with foaming waves in a clear-blue sea and rustling in the lofty treetops.

Zio and the Migration to Earth

The Angels stayed with us for a time in order to help us adjust to this new home. We had come to the planet of the "Indians": the magic, beautiful, windswept Zio that was one of the first inhabited planets in our solar system. It was not time for Earth yet! I was not born from a mother's womb, I was born from the melting of energy in Light, and so it was for all of us. We were thin, light beings, suddenly put on a physical soil, even if the density of Zio's earth was not as high as our Earth. Before I was "planted" on Zio our Earth was a glowing mass, hovering in the cosmos with other globes. There were no square or elliptical planets. The globe or the circle was the sign of the eternal origin.

We looked at each other. We observed each other. We were yin and yang. We observed the Angels. We listened and learned. We were all so beautiful! In the beginning our hair had been almost without color, and then it darkened in those early days on Zio. Our faces were no longer identical; our looks were as different as the streaming waters cascading in our new forests. When we got as far as building houses, digging in the light soil and piling up the shimmering stones, our faces were more varied. In each consciousness there was a different talent or gift. One was an artist, another was musical, and a third was a gifted craftsman. The Angels taught us how to build, how the women could weave and sew, how we could use wild animals and make them tame. There existed no evil, no quarrel about our daily bread (which became all the more substantial). There was a lot of love, joy, and fellowship.

All the time we remembered the Great Spirit, and the Angels reminded us if we forgot. At that time I was not Jan, the poet and the scoundrel standing at the gate of the Ethereal World telling stories to his Earth-friends. If you hear somebody say, "Jan went up many stairs and traveled across many levels," he is wrong. There are no staircases and no levels here, only an infinite Oneness of different Realms and sections. Study the Cosmic Map on page 3, dear reader! In the middle is the Great Spirit who floats above everything in order to supervise his creation.

"Don't pile it on too much," Shala butted in on me. "You were telling us about Zio. What happened? Did you become completely physical?"

"Yes," I answered, "but it took time, even though time didn't exist there either. We lived in a frequency without computation of time. I know that you and Zar were some of the Angels who helped us. We created no religion, although we grew in knowledge. We were true to the Great Spirit and his laws of Love.

"The glowing mass that remained on Zio was covered with mountains and soil, and the planet grew more and more physical. Our thin bodies, which until now had worked to create a planet fit to live on, also became more compact and more visible. We could touch each other. Body and soul started to work together, to laugh, to smile, and to cry – but only of joy, because sorrow was not yet invented.

"One day, when we were standing on the luscious green grass, watching the trees growing around us, we wanted to dance and sing. The trees produced fruit and the wind rustled in their leaves. Communication with the Spirits of Nature was also important on Zio. Every tree, every flower, the huge mountains, and the singing waters all had their devas, and we all talked the same language. We always communicated with them and helped each other all the time.

"We were very proud of our descent from the Great Spirit. He was our one and only ruler. We revered the dual Flame of Life and in spite of our spreading over the whole planet, our rituals resembled each other. We depended on the Sun, which for us was holy, as was the Moon. We had Sun- and Moon-dances, star-parties, and the celebration-days of the Great Spirit. We didn't know about death. Each life lasted about a thousand years and then we went through a reviving process and started all over again! We were created from living energy, and therefore we were in contact with all living energies in the whole cosmos.

"Why do I call us Indians? I want to make it easy for the reader to understand our origin, because it extends to the tribes of today. I believe you now call us Native Americans. The expression 'Indian' is quite wrong, as you probably know. It was Columbus who called us that when, in the fifteenth century, he landed on the coast of America and presumed he was in India. Our correct name is 'The People of the Sun and the Stars.' The Native Americans of today call us 'Mu luwetam,' the first people. We lived in symbiosis with the whole cosmos until the big catastrophe happened.

"A meteorite was on its way towards Zio. We were situated in the middle of our galaxy. When this happened the Earth was as physical as Zio, but had no human inhabitants. There was no chance of avoiding damage to Zio. The meteorite landed with a terrible force on one side of our unfortunate planet. We had calculated the approximate impact point and we had evacuated half our planet. Already at that time there were what you call UFOs and we got a message from the Great Spirit that those who were evacuated had to go further on and inhabit Earth. I was one of those refugees. Zio was badly hurt. The awful thrust sent it spinning many light years away to the outskirts of our galaxy. It is still there, and according to messages from Zio it has recovered its former looks, but has a gigantic sea, made by the meteorite.

"We emigrants all landed on Earth. Flora and fauna unfolded their unspoiled abundance among waters and mountains. In those days Earth had more water and fewer high mountains than Zio. One kind of animal resembled humans very closely, walking upright and having arms with hands that could grip. It had a limited intelligence and lived an unobtrusive life in a place that resembled our rain forests.

"We, created in the image of Angels, were the first human inhabitants on Earth. We tried to live as we had been taught on our own planet, and we spent a long time on reconstruction in great fellowship. But our new life wasn't completely smooth. Many of our young women were abducted by the human-like apes. Children were born and they were the mixture that became the basis of present-time humanity. We tried to make friends with this hybrid race of ape humans, but soon envy and suspicion made them our enemies. They hated us.

"Suddenly death was a fact we could not ignore. The ape humans didn't live even a hundred years. We couldn't understand that. We isolated ourselves from them and built embankments to protect us from them. Thereby ownership and hostility were established on Earth. We had been protected in our immortality and with our laws of Love – now we became weak and vulnerable. The new way of thinking brought illness and death. The lifespan diminished. The incarnation-cycle changed to the present one: a life of approximately one hundred years, and periods of living in other worlds between lives. In this way the Worlds and Realms outside the Ethereal World on the Cosmic Map were formed.

"Humans started to be humans."

4. The Lost Millennium Kingdom

It was terrible for me, the observing Jan, to hear this story about what had happened to me from the time of the birth of the Earth – and even earlier. I felt as if I still had soil from the Earth in my pocket and the amazement caused by my experiences at the Angels' School was mixed with a slight feeling of fear. I had learned so many new things, and not all of them were positive. It was bad news about planets in other galaxies which had developed strange gods. That suggested highly developed spirits with knowledge that was superior to human knowledge. They had the ability to create – and they created! They didn't work in an evil way, but they controlled energies between the planets that opened new paths for the humans.

On one of the stars of Orion reigned a monarch with a great thirst for power. His name was Godonda. He dreamed of conquering Earth, and traveled to our planet in order to subdue the tribes living there. He wanted to be looked upon as a god, and he succeeded. He frightened people until they worshiped him. In his wake followed all the minor deities – those who were the gods of various phenomena. For a long time the good Great Spirit was forgotten, because Godonda promised power and gold to those who followed him. That was not the way of the Great Spirit. He talked to people's hearts and gave them Free Will. Unconsciously Free Will was imprisoned under the rule of Godonda and people were led in the wrong direction from the beginning. Godonda also divided humans into different beliefs – for instance the Nordic Asa faith, Greek and Egyptian mythology, Judaism, and many others. Godonda hoped that the Great Spirit would lose his foothold, but he didn't. He waited, biding his time, and sent one of his great Angels to Earth in order to teach humans about the laws of Love.

Godonda's minor deities, for instance the Nordic, the Greek, and the Egyptian ones, became ambassadors for Islam, for Buddhism, and Mohammedanism. You can find gods in different cultures all over the world, but the One Eternal Spirit has been misused under the name of God – his name was taken in vain. In his name, brother attacks brother and father fights son. In God's name, crime justifies itself, and hatred and violence walk hand in hand with war and profit of all kinds.

When I lived on Earth I read many books about Creation. There must be even more of them nowadays. Books on Creation flood the market, with different opinions and different terms. While I was pondering this, Zar interrupted my thoughts.

"Stop it, my friend," he warned me in a friendly way. "The books you are talking about are true in their own way. Everything is Oneness, and all is part of this Oneness in both a cosmic and a planetary view, and therefore everything is positive! Every Truth is valid as a Truth if it originates from an honest, wise, and loving heart."

"But how on Earth can we understand, then?" I protested. "What a mess if everyone accepted everything. And what about Godonda in this Oneness?"

"You must believe what your heart tells you is true. Just imagine that the knowledge you got in the Angelic Realm is dancing a line-dance in the cosmos, where gods and humans dance together now, then, and in the future. Everybody has his place, his mission, but very few will strike your heart with Cupid's arrow."

"All this is very new, but I believe you."

"That is why Shala and I are at your side. What we have shown you in pictures and in experience is our version of the Creation, as we and you came to know it. Perhaps other consciousnesses will interpret it another way and they will tell another story. There are many colors in an opal, and one person believes it to be blue, another person finds it rose-colored, and a third one says that it is green. There are many different variations of the same thing. Don't take exception to small things; always try to see the whole. There are details everywhere, but they don't form a whole before they are put together. For you, millions of years were a very varied sea of feelings, light- and sound-experiences.

Go on now, with your memories from the first time on Earth."

"I remember that we lived in villages where we had a 'mother' and a 'father' who helped us with everything. These 'parents' kept their ethereal shape longer than us. Our lives lasted 1000 years as long as we were not victims of the ape humans and did not catch any of the diseases that are nowadays human peculiarities: hatred, envy, jealousy, greed, lust for power, etc. The inner group of The People of the Sun and the Stars had to meet secretly in holy places that were hidden in caves or underground. We could never be sure that the ape humans or wild animals would not attack us – but it was easier to handle wild animals than wild human beasts.

"Some of the original holy places where we assembled still remain on Earth. You can find them in Canada, New Mexico, Peru, the Andes, the Himalayas, the North Pole, and the South Pole. Sea and land have changed and moved, but these places remain approximately where they always were. We have left memories that humans cannot yet interpret. In the future there will be discoveries.

"When a human reached the limit of 1000 years, he or she had to go through a ritual before 'refreshing.' If the person could pass the tests that were imposed they would continue into the next 1000-year period. More and more of us couldn't make it. These we called 'emigrants.' I never thought I would be one of them – not until my 'fall' was a fact.

"The eternal female always captivated me, captured me, and led me into a butterfly-dance that sometimes ended badly. Perhaps the boy Jan was already awake in me in those ancient times, because one day, when I was walking in the forest near my home, I caught sight of a human girl with long, golden hair. I realized she was a mixture of ape and human. She was very beautiful, sitting near the brook, washing her feet. When I passed very near her she playfully splashed water on me. It ended badly. Did she seduce me or I her? I hardly had time to think before she disappeared like a flash before she had told me her name. I felt bad about it and never told anybody. I filed it in my subconscious as if it never happened. I loved the sunny family I had at home; the whole group of loving people who shared the same ancient wisdom.

"Later on – some months, maybe a couple of years – I met the golden-haired girl again. She was sitting beside the same brook in the same forest as the last time we met. Again I felt a consuming desire for her. Again she awakened my male primitive instincts, something between making love and fighting. I tried to get rid of this terrible current that boiled inside me when I saw her half-naked body. The current grew to a sea of lovesick feelings, hotter than hell, filled by an insatiable hunger – a crazy current, flowing like lava from a volcanic eruption, beyond all sensible warnings. Soon we were lying on the grass in each other's arms. My lust was satisfied, but after that she suddenly disappeared just like last time. This time she came back. She had a small child in her arms: a white-skinned boy with rosy cheeks and heavenly blue eyes. 'My son!' I thought. 'My son with this lovely, wild woman?'"

I had no time to enjoy this before the whole picture vanished and I slowly floated towards the temple of the 1000-year ritual. The Day of Judgment for me!

"You've failed," were the sad words I heard. "Why did you make the same mistake again? Somewhere in the desert behind our forests the woman with the golden hair lives with your son. You must find them. You don't belong to our group any longer. You will never be a thousand years old, only one hundred. You are vulnerable, remember! You may die earlier, as man on Earth often does, but that will be your experience. Remember, my son, that we love you very much, but you will have to leave us. One day you will meet us again in another World of Light and then you can decide for yourself what you wish to do with your eternal life. Until then, farewell!"

Lucifer created a new world for himself when he was rejected. It was my turn now. But my world was not evil, only filled with strong Earthly feelings: the wild fever of sexuality and the cold grave of disappointment and self-contempt. I started walking and tried to be the happy, careless fellow, the clown and joy-bringer I once was. But underneath the coarse jokes and laughter was a lonely, sad wanderer.

My journey was lonely and adventurous. I still had my memory of the other world, the World of Light, and it hurt. I looked for the truth.

I looked for Golden-hair and the blue-eyed baby. After many years, I found her. She was living with an ape-man. She had many children with him and my son was no longer among them. I wanted to go on looking for him, but the ape-man killed me. He represented evil and jealousy – the Godonda-power. That was my first death, before all the other thousand ones.

I lost the Millennium Kingdom and had to wait until the present time on Earth to get back my immortality in a time that doesn't exist. When I went back to the Angels' School, where I was shown all this, I must admit that it was a shock to be informed about my failure at such an early stage of my "heavenly journey."

The Tale of Toja

I journeyed through many kingdoms, some of them dark, some of them light. In most of them the inhabitants were calm and hard-working, with a chief or a king as leader. Later on these small kingdoms were called tribes.

As an itinerant, I heard many strange stories. There are various stories of the Flood, not only about old Noah or Gilgamesh, the Sumerian epic, but also many others. These stories prove that many great floods, throughout Earth's history, really happened. I loved one of these legends – about a woman, for a change. It is a beautiful and sad story that shows the triumph of male self-esteem as such an unfair one!

When this story begins, The People of the Sun and the Stars had already established their kingdoms on Earth, thousands of years ago. The big disruption had started. People went too far in their envy and desire for power, and were led to evil and crime. The fight for power was at its worst in a large kingdom, surrounded by the sea.

In this kingdom lived a woman called Toja, with her husband and three children – two sons and one daughter. Toja was descended in a direct line from the goddess Helia's family (see page 157). She was knowledgeable about the inner world and the possibilities of its development. The inhabitants of this kingdom regarded her as a very wise woman. Her husband, Mendor, was not as gifted as she was. He was a farmer and worked with the fertile earth that gave rich harvests. Both their sons, Jap and Sojn, helped their father but they also listened to wise advice from their mother. After the birth of their little sister Ilva, their mother started to tell them remarkable stories every night. Their father dismissed these fairy tales as women's gossip, but they were actually tales where courage, strength, and love always showed the right path and where evil lurked and had to be chased away.

One day civil war came to the country. The inhabitants turned against each other, they told lies about each other and made up stories about each other. Their hatred and envy resulted in mutual informing and reporting. There were murder and executions. Toja and her family lived on the coast. One day she got an inner message telling her that the hour of reckoning was near for her people. Her inner voice demanded that she build a house that could sail on the sea, a kind of houseboat. She told her husband about the message, but he laughed and called her a crazy woman.

However Toja's sons had heard what she said to their father. They were strong and clever teenagers, both of them. Ilva was only ten years old, but all three of them helped their mother build the boat. It took them several months. Mendor scoffed at them and found the houseboat ridiculous. He assured them it would sink the moment it was put to sea.

Ilva and Toja brought the timber, and the boys were the carpenters. When the boat was ready, people from the village came to see it and smirk. Toja didn't say a word, because she knew that the boat must be launched the following morning. Then their adventures would begin. The inner voice demanded that she get a male and female animal of as many kinds as she could find, and bring them aboard. Her children helped her as always, although the villagers and her husband carried on laughing at them.

Some of the spectators tried to board the boat for a prank, but as soon as they came near it, an invisible wall prevented them. They muttered about sorcery and evil powers, but it didn't help. Those allowed aboard came aboard – no one else. Mendor hid in their old house when he saw the jealousy and repugnance of the villagers towards his family. He was safe there, because both their house and the houseboat were protected. Neither fire nor steel could damage them. At last the villagers went home, but they threatened to return the next morning.

Next morning at dawn, the whole family except Mendor boarded the houseboat. Mendor refused to go with them on such a crazy journey. But poor Toja's heart ached when she saw his lonely figure on the beach, while the boat floated on the waves as if it was created for them. Toja asked her inner counselor if she could return home to fetch her husband. The answer was yes, but it came with a serious warning. Her husband's heart was not pure enough to follow her destiny. The counselor could not prevent her from doing it out of Love, but the consequences could be completely different than what was pre-determined. Toja loved her sullen, ignorant husband and she asked her sons to return. They did so unwillingly. Ilva cried and yelled, "Mother, this will bring us bad luck! Do not return!"

But they returned and fetched Mendor. He was taken aboard against his will, shouting and kicking. At last he calmed down because of the prayers and loving words from his wife. He sat sullenly at the helm.

As soon as Mendor was on the boat, the surge appeared. Not a small surge, but a terrible wave that covered the whole horizon and drowned the whole kingdom with its enormous force. Toja's houseboat passed right through the wave to the other side. There the water was like a mirror and the boat rested peacefully on it. Toja knelt and thanked the good Power that had saved her whole family.

Mendor slept throughout. Toja carefully loosened his grip on the helm and took over. Her inner voice showed her the right direction. She steered into the rosy arms of the sunset. Everybody else on the boat fell asleep.

When they all woke up, the houseboat was floating peacefully in the shallow water near a beach. There were lots of people on the shore, waving their hands. To her surprise, Toja saw that they were the same color as her, reddish and suntanned. Her husband was as pale as the Moon, but skin colors had been very different in their former kingdom. The people on the shore honored them with flowers and aromatic herbs. They had been waiting for the boat. Toja let out all the animals from the interior of the houseboat. They caused a sensation on the beach. People screamed and laughed and sang and fell on their knees.

Toja realized that the people thought that she and her family were gods, not least because of all these rare animals. These people obviously didn't know any of the animals from Toja's former kingdom. Soon it was obvious that Toja's husband, Mendor, was looked upon as a strange god, perhaps because of his pale skin.

The family soon realized that they had landed in a place where the people were loving and friendly, with an ancient culture, but no leader. Their king had just died and there was no successor. The inhabitants thought that Mendor was sent to them as a gift from the gods. They gave him a throne of flowers, and his new subjects fussed over him and fulfilled all his wishes. Toja and the children were also met with respect and friendliness, but Mendor was the principal figure – and that suited him. He shamelessly took advantage of his new position, and all his wishes satisfied his ego.

Toja's inner voice asked her if she now understood why Mendor should have been left to the devastation of the flood. The idea was that Toja would be "the goddess," lovingly ruling and leading the lost people in the beautiful new kingdom. Her son, Jap, had inherited her ability of inner vision and was meant to succeed her. Now the energies had turned away from her because of her misguided compassion. The inner voice was very distressed, but Toja stubbornly claimed that her husband would reign well in this country. Besides, she was at his side, and she would help him lead all future projects.

But soon Toja found that her voice didn't count. Mendor chose the most beautiful women at his court and lived with them in luxury and abundance. Toja grieved, and her sons became more and more angry with their father.

Many moons had not shown their pale rays when Toja was given the message to present herself to her husband. He scrutinized her up and down and complained that she had disturbed an important meeting the other day. In reality she had surprised him when he was in bed with two women, which had really upset her. Her inner voice had asked her to take over before things got as bad as they had been in their old kingdom. The inner voice told her to reproach him for his lecherous life, and pointed out that there were necessary arrangements required in this kingdom. Mendor asked her to kneel immediately in front of his throne. She did because she loved him, unaware of his plans. She never had time to ask him for an answer before the sword of the executioner fell on her neck and separated her head from her body.

Toja, who, like Noah, had guided an ark to harbor in order to save a great many species, became a victim because she was a loving, defenseless woman. It was the first time the white man had by violence separated the right owner from his lot … the first time of many.

Toja's children had witnessed the murder of their beloved mother in silence and horror. Jap took his sister and brother and escaped through the woods up into the mountains, far away from their father's terror. Stopping at a fresh, cold mountain brook in order to drink, Jap heard his mother's voice loudly and distinctly. She said, "Go on until you see a little hut. Go inside and greet the man sitting on the earthen floor. Tell him my name and then listen to him."

The children did as their mother said and soon came upon a strange kind of hut, built in front of a huge cave. The man in the sun-colored cloak greeted them in a friendly way and with compassion. He gave them a good meal. His name was Ulon, and he was a very wise man. He lived hidden from Mendor's soldiers, because he knew that better times were to come. He loved his people but realized that they were weak and uncourageous.

The children stayed with him for many changes of the Moon and he taught Jap a secret form of combat. He made Jap a warrior – not any old warrior, but a warrior of Righteousness. When Jap was ready, Ulon sent him back to his father. Mendor was unprepared for the return of his son and called quickly for his guards. Jap just stood there, looking at his pitiful father. Mendor's head started to nod and he seemed to fall asleep, but his face was terribly contorted. At last he fell flat on the floor. He was dead. His evil power had not been strong enough against Jap's goodness.

Those who witnessed this scene proclaimed Jap as his father's successor at once. The inhabitants in this kingdom were used to obeying someone, or it would be chaos. Jap became a good ruler for his people. He called for his sister and brother and Ulon, and together this quartet made the kingdom a model for other countries. Indirectly you could say that Toja was the cause of this happy ending and that her mission at last was fulfilled.

That was the story I heard, and I think it is more interesting than Noah's Ark. This legend anyhow shows that antagonism between the red and the white races started much earlier than we have ever supposed. At the same time, we shouldn't forget that Toja's children were a mixture of red and white, which resulted in a peaceful and loving outcome.

5. The Nine Elders of Sirius

I didn't realize then that the Nine Elders would have a great influence on my destiny. They belong to the most ancient of wisdom-teachers and lived on Zio in the beginning. The Nine Elders are made up of male as well as female teachers and now live in the Central Sun on Sirius. From there they travel to whichever planets need them. Their names are not known on Earth because if they were, they would be used wrongly by those greedy for power. The Nine Elders obey only one higher Spirit: The Great, Infinite Spirit.

When I had failed in my initiation I went away, sad and lonely. Just after I had been murdered by that ape-man, I was hurled away to be born by an Earth-woman. I had to go through a lot of tests and trials, because the Nine Elders followed my destinies until the day when I could at last return to my brothers and sisters in the Ethereal World. But it was a long way to go. I didn't reach my goal until now.

In one of my lives on Earth, I had the dubious pleasure to be born the son of a king. In that life I physically met one of the Nine Elders, a remarkable woman. We can call her Helia, because she shined like a sun in a dark world. She was the one who is called "Spider-Woman" by the Native Americans. According to their faith, she is the Mother who weaves the web of Life. Helia's mission was to create light and joy on Earth. Already at that time humans used their free will to subjugate the will of their neighbors. Helia radiated love and true creative power because the Nine Elders had decided to try again with the inhabitants of Earth. Helia succeeded in her mission. Never were there such lovely buildings, never did people have such good lives and were as strong and beautiful as when she was there. She sent troops of light everywhere and I was one of her faithful commanders. I remember her wrath and her grief when we failed to create lasting light somewhere. I remember sitting with her and the other Lightcarriers in a ring, drawing up plans. She was a fantastic beauty, but her beauty was not exciting. It was more like a calm lake in the forest, where you could refresh yourself. At the same time her radiance gave us all a lot of power. Her knowledge and insight were like an infinite stream and we were the waves of that stream.

But the hunters of Power returned to Earth. The troops of Light were crushed in order to give way to quite a different kind of warrior. At last Helia realized that she couldn't do any more for her beloved Earth. The idols existed both inside and outside of the people and she couldn't fight against them anymore. My father died and I inherited his throne and started to reign as Helia had taught me. This lasted until my death, but no longer.

At the time of the destruction of Lemuria and Atlantis and the beginning of Egypt's prosperity, peace ended for the green and blossoming land we had taken care of for such a long time with Helia. Not even the Great Spirit or the Nine Elders could interfere with the work of their messengers. There were other gods in other parts of the galaxy who sent very complicated energies down to Earth in order to get people to submit to their will. One of them was Godonda. If people had tried to understand this more, the world would be a better place today. Fear was a weapon for conquering the weak. Fear made people tools of Power and still does today. Priests, not the least, contributed to this, even before they were called priests.

The old gods belong to history – that's what people believe. I remember something from my last life on Earth. When the authors had parties, we all raised our glasses and cried, "Long live the old gods! Cheers!" We were not sober enough to know that we were right! But I will come back to the gods later on. They are of interest, because they still exist and still influence people into being obedient toy-soldiers.

The Reptile People

Without me realizing, the Nine Elders guided my lives for thousands of years. Looking back on my lives and all that happened between them, I thought that it was a mess. But I was wrong, because there is a perfect order and meaning to everything. I made "journeys" here in the Angels' School that were very arduous even for a spirit. That was when I had to push my way into my former development, and it was lucky that these lessons were quite short.

I got the opportunity to enter my own Self and re-experience some very difficult karmic events during many periods of time. Between incarnations, I often made galactic journeys, and they taught me a lot. I cannot understand why it took such a long time – really until my last life on Earth – before I understood the connection between body-soul-spirit. My last "death" took me into the great cosmic system where I am now. I have met many of my sort in the Palace of Light, not far from here.

The Palace of Light resembles a magnificent hotel, with guests from the whole world. These guests have very different backgrounds, but they all have one thing in common: They are all Lightworkers. They are Angels who willingly travel to Earth or some other planet, bringing help where it is needed. You can call them invisible activists.

I would like to tell you about an adventure I had between my last life on Earth and the life before that one. I was a fraud and I lived at the card table. A well-aimed bullet ended that life and I arrived at the first foggy level, where a pretty Angel-girl met me. I was totally conscious of all my sins (and there were many!) and because my thought-processes were still limited, I presumed that I would be sent to some unpleasant place. But the Angel-girl smiled and told me that they intended to send me on an important mission.

"Can you play cards there?" I asked, full of interest. But the little Angel brought her hand back and forth in front of my eyes until I forgot all about the rascal I had been. I looked down at my body and discovered that I was wearing a white, glittering gown. The Angel took me through a huge, shimmering light and at that moment I was full of dread. Who was I? Where were they taking me?

I closed my eyes for a short while and when I opened them, I was standing in a beautiful garden. Strangely enough, I recognized the garden. It was not an Earthly memory, but I knew I had been there many times. I was in the Palace of Light on the ethereal level. I sat down on a sofa and enjoyed the lovely view of the surroundings. It was a wonderful panorama: Close by there was a sea of flowers and far away, on the horizon, there was a real sea. I caught glimpses of red and white cliffs and lush green forests …

"Welcome back, Horace!" said a friendly voice. A tall man sat down at my side. He wore a pale yellow cloak with gold embroidery. He was in his forties and had beautiful dark blue eyes and silvery-white hair. 'I was probably called Horace,' I thought, but I didn't remember a thing from my former life.

"You have been chosen for an important mission," the man continued.

"Why me?" I asked. I was surprised. Of course, I was flattered, but something was telling me that I was not worthy of so much attention.

"Don't imagine you were anyone special in your last life," he said and smiled, "because you weren't! You were a fraud and a daredevil, which is just what we need. But inside your shell, all the time there was a very good-hearted person. You cared for a poor woman who would have ended up on the streets if you hadn't helped her. She had a little son who was illegitimate, but you always maintained that there are no bastards; every child that is born is a precious stone in the forge of the Great Jeweler. You married that woman and had a son and a daughter, too. You provided for them in a dishonest manner, but you loved your family deeply and warmly. If you had money you helped everyone who asked you. When you were broke, you gave them a nice smile and exchanged a friendly word. That is why we want you to lead a mission to another planet."

"Are there more planets than Earth that are inhabited?" I asked, in wonder.

"Oh yes, many! This planet is in our galaxy and is inhabited by the Reptile People. They have started to reconnoiter Earth with a view to conquering it in the future. We definitely don't want that! And that is why we need you."

I was appalled. Of course I could not undertake such a mission. It would be better to send a diplomat who has kicked the bucket, I thought, and I said so. The man laughed.

"You are chosen for this mission," he insisted, "but first you have a lot to learn."

They put me in the Angels' School. The memory of the unprincipled but kind fraud I had been stayed with me no longer, so I managed to convince myself that my education was easy and entertaining.

I was not going alone. I worked with a group of fifty, but responsibility for success was in my hands alone. When it was time for departure I had been developing my inner and outer strength and I had been trained in different forms of protection. My legs were trembling when we entered the spaceship that would take us to the alien planet.

We were met by a group of Reptile People when we landed. I had seen pictures of them in school, so I was prepared. Yet, reality was frightening. I saw that my companions thought the same, but now it was important not to show any fear. I went straight to the man at the head of the reptiles. Imagine a crocodile standing upright and you get some idea of his height. His gold- and green-shimmering skin was like leather. His head was almost human, but not particularly attractive. His golden-green eyes were sloped slightly, with heavy, protruding, scaly eyelids resembling sun awnings. He had a broad mouth with thick lips, and his nose was short and wide, with large nostrils. None of the reptiles had hair, but some skulls were rounded in a human way. Others heads were long and narrow, like the old Egyptians.

"Hail in the name of Love and Light!" I had been instructed to salute them in this way.

"Welcome in the name of Dendra!" was the answer, sounding short and metallic. I knew that Dendra was the god of this remarkable people.

"My name is Rok, and I will guide you to the palace," he added.

"Our ruler, Murq, wants to see you at once, alone."

"But I am part of a group of representatives from different worlds on our frequency," I objected.

"If you don't want to anger our ruler, please come alone!" was the answer. "We will take good care of your friends as long as they don't behave like enemies."

Rok looked grim, and threat vibrated in the air. The Reptile People came nearer and made a circle around my men. I swiftly told my group that they had to wait for me and I followed the big reptile man across a bridge over a river that looked quite Earth-like. The color of the water differed slightly from ours. It was transparent but had a deep blue-green color which must be ideal for camouflaging the Reptile People. Rok turned around and smiled at me.

"We live very much in the water," he said. "It's good to be invisible if the enemy is near."

I asked him who his enemy was, but I got no answer. His broad, scaly back looked safe in this strange rocky landscape. Here and there were small patches of grass, but no other vegetation. The ground was sometimes covered with thick, thistle-like leaves. Rok picked some and chewed them with great pleasure. He indicated to me to follow his example. I tasted the leaves and they actually had a nice taste. They contained a liquid that reminded me of honey.

The palace was in a cliff. In front of it was an open space. I admitted to myself unwillingly that the front of the palace was very beautiful. It was hewn out of the red rock, and in its center was a huge doorway, decorated with gold and gems. Beautiful reliefs framed it. The windows on both sides had reliefs that probably represented the history of the Reptile People.

I would have loved to study them more closely, but Rok seemed impatient and waved me on.

At last I would meet this Murq, something for which I had been preparing for a long time. We went through several beautiful doors and saw Reptile People running about with various things in their claws. The ceiling height was impressive but the last door was low and made out of simple wood. Rok opened it and pushed me in. I was standing in front of Murq, the reptile ruler. I had heard many stories about him and his powerful planet. He had been a successful conqueror in many cosmic wars.

"You are welcome!" I heard him say, while my brain was registering the normal, yet unusual, surroundings. He was sitting at a sculptured table, on which a dinner was served. I never imagined that reptile faces were so different! This being looked royal and his expression was nearly jovial. He indicated to me to sit down right opposite him.

"You're from Earth, I presume?" he asked. "That is very interesting for us. Earth-people visit us very seldom."

"Well, I'm not exactly terrestrial any longer," I muttered. "My mission is to ask you not to invade Earth. People must be allowed to develop their own way, and because they have got free will, like you, they must learn to use it properly. They can't if they are forced to obey you. Threat creates fear, and fear solves no problems. It makes the problems grow. Do you want an Earth of problems, with prisoners who hate and scoff at you?"

"You are a wise messenger," Murq said and smiled. "I have to tell you that we have studied Earth for a long time and have come to the conclusion that it is a dying planet. We have not planned an invasion, but a rescue."

"Really, Earth is not dying," I protested. "She is still beautiful and has lots of natural assets, but I can tell you that her inhabitants have changed."

"I know, I know," the ruler interrupted irritably. "Humans have succeeded in ruining their Earth deep into the bedrock – in a short time. They have also ruined themselves and each other with free will. It will be worse in the future. If they had had a strong leader and strong laws this destruction would never have occurred."

"Nothing will improve if you rule over them," I objected angrily. "And actually you would frighten them with your appearance, which differs very much from theirs."

"They would have to get used to us! We are not evil, young man. We are not going to kill you and eat you!" he joked. He was laughing, but his eyes glittered strangely. "We just want to teach you to live in peace and respect authority. We are actually a peace-loving people, even if we have sometimes been involved in wars originating from other parts of the cosmos. And, we are a creative people as well. Have you seen what artistic heights we have achieved? We can teach you to develop enormous talents in various genres of art."

"We already have plenty of good art on Earth," I answered, "and the Great Spirit asks you to renounce this project. If Earth has not changed in a positive way within the course of a couple of hundred years from now, the Great Spirit will discuss this with you again. He knows about your highly skilled art and culture, but your whole planet is full of mountains. You cannot develop without blasting half your planet. He suggests that you start developing your inner selves and he would gladly supply teachers."

"Thanks, we don't need any," was the cool answer. "We don't obey the laws of the Great Spirit, but we will listen to them if they are reasonable and if Dendra gives his acknowledgment. We must listen to the desires of our god Dendra. In this case he has given us an ultimatum. There are things we want to find out about humans and we are going to do that. Since your delegation consists of humans that have developed on a higher level in the worlds of the Great Spirit, Dendra has a proposal for you. If we might keep your delegation here, we promise not to invade Earth now. You can return with this message. Your friends will be perfectly safe, but we need them. This offer is non-negotiable. I, Murq, ruler of the Reptile Planet, have spoken."

The door behind me opened. I bowed to the ruler, who returned to his meal. I could not discuss this any further with him, and now I had the disagreeable task of presenting Murq's proposal to my colleagues in a discreet way.

When I told them, there was silence. A significant silence. My colleagues were sitting together in a pleasant drawing-room in the palace. They looked comfortable, but tall guards stood to attention at the doors. There was no chance of escape. After a short while one of my men, who looked open and kind, rose and spoke.

"Is there anyone who will report for duty voluntarily?" he asked. "We all have the privilege of returning to the Worlds of the Great Spirit sooner or later. Our whole Earth, where we once lived and loved, is in danger of being captured and perhaps changed in a negative way by the reptiles. What are our ethereal lives compared to the whole population of Earth? We are already dead; we cannot die again! If we share our knowledge with this people they may release us after a while. We will help Mother Earth while sharing our ancient wisdom with the reptiles."

This was a true gentleman talking. I embraced him and then asked if they were all prepared to stay. At first there was silence. Then, one by one, all hands were raised. Tears ran down my cheeks when Rok took me back to the waiting ship.

"In the name of Dendra," he whispered in my ear, "I promise nothing bad will happen to your friends. I can manage the ruler!"

It was sad but good tidings I took to the Ethereal World. But the Reptile People kept their promise. They have not yet invaded Mother Earth. But no one from my delegation has returned either. Only Horace returned to Earth to be reborn as the farm boy Jan.

6. In the Angels' School

I underwent trial after trial after my last life, after experiencing the Akashic Records, and decided to stay in the Ethereal World. My goal is tough and far from being reached. But because time no longer exists, I believe I have eternal life ahead of me. And now we will continue with the teaching in the Angels' School.

Shala informed me of the first trial. It was about longing, I mean longing to be back on Earth. If I felt that way, it was too early for me to proceed. Longing is such a common word on Earth. We always long to be another person, to conquer hearts, to earn a lot of money, to travel to foreign countries, to be loved…. We are always longing for someone or something, and on Earth longing can be creative. A Swedish poet wrote these lines: "Yearning is my inheritance, the castle in the valleys of loss."

My pretty teacher escorted me to a room in the Angels' School where I had never been before. The room was circular, like a tower room.

"It is a tower room." Shala smiled. "Didn't you notice that this house has a tower with a golden roof? We all love it!"

I'm sorry to say that I had looked more at Shala than at the school building. She read my thoughts as usual, laughed, and disappeared from the room with a sly expression on her face. When she closed the door you could not see it any longer, it had become one with the wall. I hoped I wouldn't feel claustrophobic!

I sat down in an armchair in the middle of the room. It was a swivel chair. A pleasant bluish light made me think of a blue cupola. It suddenly smelled like Spring and a light breeze blew through the room. Suddenly the plain walls started to show a magnificent panorama. I went round and round in my chair and there were glades of hepaticas and slopes of wood anemones on mossy ground covered with needles and cones. The wind rustled the trees – fir trees, birches, alders, and rowans – common trees in a Swedish forest. I heard the babbling of a brook and I could see it flow in a deep furrow near an old, rounded, overgrown country road. Uprooted trees raised their animal-like, straggling shapes above the moss and played with the imagination of the observer. I could feel the wonderful smell of Spring, of damp soil, and of growing vegetation. I could see a bear watching me from his den and a fox running out of his burrow, with a tail of pups close behind. The birds fed their nestlings, and a buzzard nestled high up in a pine crown. The elk majestically walked between the tree trunks while the white rump of a deer flickered by through a thorn-brake.

I lived Spring, I breathed Spring from my swivel-chair. Just as my longing for a Swedish Spring morning in the forest held my heart in its grip, the scene changed very slowly. I was fascinated to see how my favorite flowers budded and opened in slender grass-tufts in early Summer: cowslip, bitter vetch, buttercup, saxifrage, clover, marguerite, and forget-me-not. I experienced the scents of Midsummer and haymaking, flowers, weeds, sun, and rain. I was in the middle of it all, enjoying it and longing for it! When the Summer around me faded and the leaves turned red and gold, I felt my pulse quicken. I always loved early Autumn with its clear air and plentiful sunshine, glittering in moist red-gold colors. On a sunny Autumn day you can see the nuances of a red maple leaf, so beautifully designed and delicately veined.

I was disturbed in my reverie by a slow snowfall. Big snowflakes fell on the red leaves and covered the ground in shimmering white drifts. I saw a kick-sledge at the corner of a house and a couple of skis were ready to be used with their poles in the new, soft snow.

I followed the seasons and I really enjoyed it – I longed for everything I saw! But when this Winter landscape disappeared and the blue walls in the tower room enclosed me like a heavenly cape, I realized that, after all, the beauty of Earth also existed where I was now. I lived in the dwellings of beauty, in the origin of its sister, which is called Earth.

New pictures appeared on the wall. They whispered a memory-song and I was deeply moved. All the good and beautiful moments from my last Earth-life were included, all the favorite places of my memory.

Were they still there in the valleys of loss?

That was what Shala asked me when she entered the tower-room. I don't know how long I had been sitting there, swiveling round and round in the chair, afraid to miss anything. I had smelled all kinds of things, including freshly-brewed coffee and fresh-baked bread. I had heard whispered words and I had seen myself and my near ones and dear ones, and heard their happy, friendly voices. There were no dark memories, maybe in order to give me the impression that I had always had a happy life. I had read poems with my friends and visited places I loved.

The claws of longing ought to have torn a hole in my heart, but I looked calmly at Shala and said, "If this was a trick to entice me back to another life on Earth, it was unsuccessful. I admit that I enjoyed it, that I loved every second of the images, aromas, and meetings with friends. All the time I was thinking how beautiful Earth is and how pure its Nature. But you only showed me nice things. What I saw was a dream – you picked the beautiful moments of my life: true ones, but so small when you compare them to the negative parts. No thanks! I will refrain from living on Earth again, however beautiful it is. You can't live down there without the negative or even evil being caught up in the web of your life. Here and now is *life!* Earth is the most difficult test of them all."

Shala nodded thoughtfully. "'As above, so below' is what humans say. But they're only right in their own limited context. The lasting beauty, love, and goodness are to be found here. The trial enters inside of you and creates either despair, longing, or worry. But it might also be a confirmation, as in your case. You come out of the ordeal well, dear Jan!"

The Dual Flame

After the trials, my courses continued at the Angels' School. I felt that after having passed my examination I was moved from the first stage to the middle stage. The last stage was yet only a dream, a longing, a vision. But Zar and Shala helped me to understand. Zar taught and told stories, and Shala explained and elucidated what was difficult to grasp. Sometimes I was the only pupil, sometimes we were several. Many times I thought I recognized some of the other pupils, but I never had the chance to ask them. After the classes we were given other tasks. Sometimes we watched plays or listened to music, sometimes we danced, and we often sang. We also studied in the big observatory or in one of the technical departments. It was all very varied and very interesting.

"We have talked about gods that exist in so many different forms in the innumerable religions on Earth," Zar said. "Soon we'll travel around in the Worlds here, but before that I will explain a little more of these beings and why they are called 'gods.' You have learned about the Dogons, haven't you? They are a people in Africa. Many thousand years ago, beings from Sirius landed there in order to repair their spaceship. They stayed for a while with the Dogons and taught the tribe a lot of things. They were called 'gods' because they came from space and disappeared the same way. To this day on Earth, the Dogons still tell the legend of the gods from Sirius. That's just one example of endless similar stories. Aliens from space, from other planets, galaxies, and universes, were much more common about 5000 years ago, and that is why stories like these remain on people's lips. They became part of their dreams and wishes. The help that these 'gods' gave their brothers and sisters on Earth was called 'miracles.'

"To meet people's different wishes and prayers for help, the 'gods' were given a number of qualities. It was simpler that way. The 'gods' had to represent the qualities of the humans, good and bad. They were the 'gods' of love, wealth, prosperity, war, health, the Sun, and the Moon. They were split up into thousands of names. These 'gods,' in reality, are living in the best of health on their cosmic home planets. Sometimes the messages and thoughts from peoples who worship them reach them, and then they can send back vibrations or energies which may achieve a 'miracle.' I'm sorry to admit that this kind of contact between humans and 'gods' can bring about as many bad things as good ones."

I asked about the Central Sun. Are there several Central Suns? The answer was yes. Every galaxy has its own Central Sun, Zar said, independent of how many other suns and moons that are in orbit around it. A Central Sun is not what we call a sun, because it is not physical. You cannot look at it with binoculars. It's more of a radiation of combined power, which constitutes the true power-source for all the planets and stars of the galaxy. If exploited correctly this power can generate a tremendous amount of energy, and as such we use it for different purposes – for instance, propulsion of our ships, because it contains dynamic kinetic energy. This enormous power source is situated on a physical planet or star in the galaxy. In our galaxy the Central Sun is located on Sirius.

"Is there any connection between Duals and the Central Sun? Do they exist there?" I asked.

"No, my friend, that is not correct!" Zar smiled. "Every human being has a Dual of the other sex, and these two are united here, either in the Ethereal or in the Astral World. This union may take its time. On Earth you have really confused things ridiculously. You talk about Duals, Twin Souls, Twin Flames, and so on. Every other woman walks around hoping for a Twin Soul. Many psychics shamelessly talk about Twin Souls, who will crop up within the lifetime of the client. This may lead to labeling a partner wrongly as their Twin Soul. Consequently both partners may expect too much from each other and they will probably have a hard time playing 'the dream-prince' or 'the dream-princess.'

"Of course you have a Dual! Of course you will be united with him or her. Of course you may find a soul-partner in your Earth-life, but that has nothing to do with your Dual. Of course you love on this side of the bridge too, between then and now. But that love is so great, so all-embracing, and so pure, that you can only be a small part of it. That's how we love each other here. You can't compare that to Earth-love."

"I haven't met my Dual yet," I said. "She has remained on Earth and I am faithfully waiting for her. Is it not the intention that male and female must be in balance in every human being? For me, the male has always outweighed the female. But the most important thing for my Jan-life was that I had my muse. I talked to her for hours and these conversations became my books. Many times I left my work and the claims of my family just to be with her, my inspiration. She always lived in my head and I allege that she was the worst rival a wife could ever have, because she was with me in bed and in all intimate moments of my life. She came with me on my morning walk and sat with the family in the evening. I see my muse as an Angel, a divine apparition, a ringing cymbal, a singing fanfare. But sometimes she was an advocate of sorrow and suffering. She was my mirror, my recklessness, my melancholy, my everything. And I haven't lost her, because death could not part us. She still lives in the thin tissues that are now my head."

"But dear friend, she is not your Dual, she is your genius," Zar was now really amused. "The Dual is your opposite. Together you become the negative and the positive pole that makes the lamp burn. You are the two faces of Love: The one who lives on Earth only feels Earthly love while the one who stays here feels the All-love. Is that difficult to understand? Both feel longing, the longing for each other, the feeling of incompleteness. That can only be satisfied in one of the Worlds on the other side of the Portal. Duals that are united here – something that often happens – have the free will to proceed along together. They can choose, but not without a counselor."

"Proceed?" I asked.

"Yes, I mean proceed in their development. They can also travel together. That depends upon their wishes and our guidance. But I cannot unveil everything that happens here. The soul must have some remaining secrets to find out."

"You talk much of free will. Please explain more to me!" I asked him. "'The Duals can if they want to ...' you say. Do you keep your free will completely when you have passed the border? The inhabitants on Earth were given free will as an experiment, a test of how they would cope with it. I have heard that free will doesn't exist anywhere else in our galaxy. But now that I have regained my full memory, I remember we had free will on Zio. Did we bring it with us? And what can you do with free will when you are imprisoned on Earth? The soul is held captive in a body that can be somewhat unpleasant, and free will is often not at all free. Free wills intersect each other like shining swords from birth to the grave. It is no longer a question of free will, but who has the strongest will and who has the power over all the weak-minded wretches crawling in the mire of life. Am I right?"

"The children of Earth had their chance of free will, anyhow," Zar objected. "It's everyone's business how to handle it. Don't be so negative about it, Jan! There is also another explanation. After the fall of Lucifer, the Cosmic Council and the Nine Elders worried about what he would be up to next. Nowhere in the galaxy was there any question of limiting free will. That didn't happen. But on certain planets there are rulers who oppress their subjects, and Lucifer wanted power. Most of all, his dark creations wanted to strike and conquer. It is will against will in our galaxy, in fact, in our whole Universe. It's not only a global problem, it's universal. And I ask you: Is there really anyone with a free will? It is only a turn of phrase, nothing else.

"The Great Spirit gave every energy-seed an individual soul that wouldn't submit to anything else but the laws of Love and Truth. How these souls conducted their innate gift was up to them. You're also confusing Order, that is regulated by Law, with free will. There is a Cosmic Origin, from which we all descend. The Origin doesn't seek to suppress, it guides every single soul through its inner Self. Don't confuse inner and outer will! The inner will is connected to the Origin and only acts in accordance with Cosmic Order. There are so many false doctrines on Earth, and among them I consider free will the worst. The outer will is the one that is easy to manipulate.

"You must realize that on Earth the law of strength is valid and this has conquered free will. If you revolt against those in power, free will is of no help. You will only be dragged into the dirt and slaughtered. Your 'enlightened' Earth is darkened by ignorance and a strong urge to profit from it. Mother Earth has her free will like all other planets, but in order to control it you need power, the power of Love. Her power is no longer enough. It will soon be transformed into wrath.

"My dear Jan, may I suggest that we walk on further into the Worlds."

7. The No Man's World

I can only convey to my readers a small part of what I learned here. If I told everything I have learned here it would be shelves and shelves of books containing the wisdoms of the Origin – but the time is not right for that yet. Perhaps you're wondering how I developed from being an irresponsible rogue in one life and a poor farm boy in another. These dark and hard lives would not necessarily provide an entrance-ticket to Heavenly glory – but you do not know what lies behind all this. I didn't know myself why I had the grace to be taught by the high Spirits in the Ethereal World. I didn't feel worthy when I had seen my Akashic Record.

Zar continued, "We don't judge the details of your lives. We look at the wholeness of the individual from the Beginning until the present. We look at the flow of love, the thirst for truth and wisdom, and the purity of your intentions. We accept your failures, your anger, and your grief as shadows from your Higher Self. The shadows must be there too. You cannot fully appreciate Light without them. In all your lives you were a Seeker and acted accordingly. You always knew that your subconscious hid secrets of light and love.

"When you were a warrior, a rogue, one who hated his surroundings, when you thought yourself guided by dark forces, the first human being from Zio was shining through. You lived through a fall like Lucifer's. Lucifer again works with his brothers. The same goes for you. Your fall caused the imperfection of your body, the weakness you share with your brothers and sisters: desire. Sometimes your old love-force has been evident in your actions, consciously or unconsciously. Your subconscious has always referred to the Source, even if you didn't listen. Every time you have crossed the border you have been with us and worked with us, mostly from the Astral World. Not until now have you started your education in the Ethereal World. You are ready for it now."

"Did my visit to the Reptile World start from the Astral World?" I asked.

It was Shala who answered, "Oh yes. You have had many missions in the realms of the Astral World, but all the time we were behind you and helped you, even if you didn't know."

I pondered over this and at the same time a door opened for me – no, several doors. One of them is the Cosmic Map for life after life. (See the Map on page 3.) It is time to guide the reader around the enormous, eternal spiral that rules our galaxy. When you press it together it is easier to understand it, because then the spiral forms a map of all Worlds in the afterlife. It is like a beautifully cut gemstone, with more facets that you can ever imagine. When you die you are reborn to a realm somewhere in the Worlds on that map. That's the birth to the real reality. After that, when you are sent back to the Earth-school, you choose your parents and environment based on the experiences of your former Earth life. I chose to be born as farm boy Janne. I won't do that again! It is not necessary. The time of the dandelions is over, even though it has been worthwhile. The light down is whirling in the air and will soon be used to line birds' nests or perhaps become part of the soil. My cycle is complete. Now "back" is not my concern any more, only "forwards."

I invite the reader to join me on my long journey through the different Worlds. The journey won't let you know everything, because each person's "everything" is not identical. Take my hand and walk safe by my side. You will see new Truths unfolding in front of your surprised eyes. Remember, nothing that I tell you can be proven until you have crossed the light border yourself. On Earth, hard core evidences are all that count. The limited world view you have created on Earth is far from the Truth. It is an escape, since it contains too many "truths" that in fact are lies. It will be hard for the people on Earth to acknowledge the Truth that resides on this frequency. I recommend that you listen to your own inner voice. Only then you will be able to find the Truth!

In the ultimate fog, the thin, aromatic smoke and the vague contours are where most souls end up when they have crossed the border. In that moment everybody needs help. No Man's World extends around the second outer circle of the Cosmic Map. (I will talk about the ultimate circle later on.) It has earth to walk upon and a mild air to breathe. Many people do not understand that they are dead. They seek their roots on Earth and rove about without finding them. I will illustrate this with a few true examples:

Five men were in deep meditation in a cottage in Halland. (Halland is a Swedish county.) Suddenly an old lady appeared to one of the men. She seemed totally confused. She was crying desperately.

"Where am I?" she asked. "Why am I not at home? And who are you?" The man told her that she was dead. She didn't want to believe him. She said that her name was Anna Albrektsson and that she lived in the South of Sweden. She had been a dressmaker but was now retired. She thought she had gone astray. She had gone out early in the morning and it was very foggy. She was going to visit her brother Aron. She met some people in the fog, but nobody had answered her or noticed her. She was worried, because she had pains in her heart.

The man explained carefully how she had left her body on Earth and that she now was walking over a crossing for souls. Then she asked why she suddenly could distinctly see the five men and talk with one of them. She must be on Earth – or else were the five men spirits? Well, explained the man, they had contacted Anna in order to help her. They talked for a while about Heaven and Earth, but Anna stubbornly refused to believe she was dead. Suddenly Anna's mother appeared. Anna was dismayed; she knew her mother was dead. When her mother asked her to go with her, the old woman asked the man how she could meet her dead mother. There was some discussion, but at last she went with her mother's spirit. All five men perceived a light going through the room.

The next example is of a man who woke up in the middle of the night and couldn't get back to sleep. He went into the kitchen to get a sandwich, but stopped at the door. The kitchen was full of people who wailed and seemed very confused. They were not quite physical, but he could see and hear them very plainly. He tried to comfort them and asked them who they were, but he got no answers. After a while they disappeared. The following day he heard that a bus accident had happened nearby and many people had died.

Both of these events took place in the 1960s. I think situations of this kind happen every day. The bridge between Earth-life and No Man's World is thin and fragile. Sudden death can bring both physical pain and confusion before a person is taken care of. The silver cord, which I call the leash, is still there and is tied to Earth, even if the body has been destroyed by fire or explosion. But usually help comes very fast. Angels are on guard everywhere inside and outside No Man's World.

The first thing I saw after death was, as I told you before, a fog full of shapes. They were like shadows, I could see no features and they moved in a nervous, jerky, and worried way. I was aware of an aromatic scent. The fog was not unpleasant, just different.

The tunnel that generally appears directly after the moment of death always leads to a light. The light is there, whether you run through the fog or stay there. Not everyone dares to walk towards the light. Not everyone can see the Guardian Angels. Imagine that thousands of people come into the fog every day. Maybe ten of them go directly towards the light. The others stay in the world of shadows until they understand that they also belong to the light. Guardian Angels are there all the time.

Many people won't accept that they are dead. If they died in a hospital they believe they are still suffering there. We have hospitals that treat these people. It may take some time to get them to realize that they have passed the border and now are completely well, but they don't always understand their situation.

There are also groups of people who belong to each other as soon as they come here and who recognize each other and are happy to reunite. Sometimes people search in the fog without knowing what they are looking for. The Guardian Angels try to get them to understand, but they won't listen. It may take a long time before such a group is ready to cross the bridge.

It is different with children. Do you remember the fairy tale about the Pied-Piper from Hamelin? He came to a village that was plagued by rats. He put all the rats to flight with his flute, but the villagers didn't show any gratitude. Then he assembled all the children in the village and disappeared with them. We have a mischievous, jolly musician here too. He is a real Peter Pan who swiftly and lovingly takes all small children's souls to the Astral World. When they arrive they are given help and guidance by Angel-teachers, educated for this task. Children are wise and easy to care for. They often continue with what they were doing before they went down to Earth. You can see (on the Cosmic Map) that they are near to Nature and animals. Every child has a task. They never have time to get bored. No child is born evil on Earth! All children are full of love and they have the memory of the light from where they descended. That memory remains at various periods of their lives. But evil goes its own way; it avoids the clean minds of children. If a young soul is weak and easily affected, a bad energy might penetrate it after a time.

There are groups of Light that work together through many lives. They descend to Earth together and they have a common goal. They may not find each other or realize that they have a goal. No one takes the memory of previous lives with them, yet there is some kind of subconscious memory in everybody. Do you recognize this expression: "Haven't we met before? I sort of recognize you ..." But they have not met in their present life and do not recognize each other from this life.

There are groups who meet because they have important missions. They often recognize each other and feel at ease with one another. There are other groups who are not positive, for instance the drug addicts who come to No Man's World. Some of them do not want to be cured, and when they descend to Earth to the next life they repeat the same hell as last time. It is tragic, but as long as their will is caught in this terrible "disease" we can do nothing. We never use force. People must come into the Light of their own free will.

I am not religious. I wasn't when I lived on Earth, and I am not religious now either. You must see my experiences from the beginning of this book as unembroidered autobiography. In my last years on

67

Earth I studied spiritualism, but found that it only gave me a superficial knowledge of what happens after death. After that I became acquainted with books by psychics like Helena Blavatsky and Alice Bailey and I felt miles nearer the truth. Not until I was reborn here did I understand that all I had been dreaming about was only a faint echo of the eternal cosmic spiritual Truth. No one needs to believe me. In fact, how could someone believe me if they had no memory of life after death?

I have to tell you a little about the belief that near ones and dear ones always meet you at the crossing. Most religions assert this, but spiritualism takes this belief another step. They maintain to the mourners that they have contact with the dead person, and they describe how he looks and is dressed, which causes lots of tears. This is not good at all. Besides, even when a serious medium acts as an intermediary of words and pictures from the dead person, the souls of the deceased are brutally torn down to Earth unless they are developed enough to project themselves. This is quite unusual. In the beginning of my occult studies I was fascinated by this, but I soon realized that souls weren't happy with this contact because they had the opportunity to develop towards the Light. This opportunity is always delayed by grief and woe and even more by trying to recall their spirits.

If a soul comes to No Man's World and demands to meet its relatives, this demand is decided from case to case. It's not certain that the relative is still on the other side any more. He or she might have gone back to Earth in a new incarnation. Sometimes a soul thinks he has come directly to Heaven. He must then be convinced that Heaven is a vague expression for a new kind of being, where you learn to acquire the virtues you lacked in your Earth-life and to overcome bad habits and wrong thinking. Bad and evil people keep their ideas until they listen to the Angels. If a soul has stolen something or has ruined poor people, he will lose riches and regain them in an eternal cycle until he tires of it and wants to go further.

There are waiting stations in No Man's World where, for example, those who have committed suicide may live until a decision is made about their future development. They may have to return to Earth very soon, because they must complete the time they have taken from their cosmic destiny.

We won't stay any longer in No Man's World. I propose that we leave this foggy part of the cosmos and proceed to the infinite number of Realms in the Astral World.

8. The Realms of the Astral World

The Astral World is an inexhaustible subject. It is thrilling and mysterious. This time I didn't live there, but I have been there a lot at other times. I well remember visiting the Realms of Dreams with Shala and Zar. I had told them enthusiastically about one of the best things I know: Swedish Midsummer with all its beauty.

"Imagine," I used to say, "when we raise the Maypole at home. The men puff and groan, their smell of sweat mixed with illicitly distilled alcohol, and joyous shouts blend with swearing from the public, before the pole stands there like a young bride, adorned with beautiful flowers and leaves. The gaudy colors in the girls' dresses gleam only as much as the expectation in their eyes. Where is my loved one? Will I meet him on the meadow in the cool of a Midsummer's evening? Accordion and violin produce happy tones, sometimes pure, but filled with sorrow, sometimes cheerful, yet fleeting like the swallow on the roof of the barn. From the hay-barn you hear tittle-tattle, and most important of all is the scent of Summer, Summer, Summer …"

The Realms of Dreams

My two friends had heard this so many times that they were sick to death of it. Imagine my surprise when we entered the Realms of Dreams and were suddenly standing in front of a real Swedish Midsummer-pole, with all the celebration, music, laughing, singing, and cheering! I went totally wild, like the young man I once was on Earth, and I flung myself into the dance, put my arms around the first slender waist I saw, and danced round and round in a reckless whirl. My dancing partner had long blond curls, eyes like bluebells, and a mouth like a red clover, awash with honey for the eager cavalier. A living, warm, young female body in a summer meadow was full of forbidden promise! I took her hand and we danced together out of the circle towards the distant forest. Suddenly we had to stop because a stream playfully babbled in front of our feet. A naked, laughing man was sitting on a rock in the swirling water. He was playing a violin: It was Neckan, the water sprite! I lost my grip on the girl and Neckan laughed louder and louder and ... suddenly Shala was there, embracing me. Zar was supporting me, because my ethereal legs were trembling and wouldn't obey me.

"You wanted to have a real Swedish Midsummer, so we let you!" Zar smiled. "It might be a good introduction to the land of chimeras. Just don't lose your foothold here, because there are dark depths into which you can fall. We will be traveling in the land of dreams where there's a lot to learn."

"This Realm doesn't just offer us our own creations, like your Midsummer," Shala added. "We are now in the astral suburbs. The inner edges brush against the wonderful Nature World. We will start here in the outskirts where dreams and fantasies are located. We are as light as feathers here – so much is created here, and it is never negative. Creation can stop directly if the creator doesn't want to proceed and is happy with what has been achieved."

"The Dreamworld plays a very important role in many ancient cultures on Earth," Zar interrupted. "The Indians believe in it and also the Aborigines, who regard it as one of the original sources of wisdom from time immemorial."

"Do you mean normal dreams?" I asked. "I never remember what I dream. I never understood what the Indians meant by their dreamtime. Apparently, they move to another dimension of thinking or daydreams, which becomes real for them. Is that right?"

"Dreamtime is a special Realm here," Zar answered. "Perhaps Dreamtime sounds wrong in your language, but that's what it is, and it does not necessarily have any connection with dreams at night. You have to attain a special state of raised consciousness. Then you let the soul travel on its own journeys in Dreamtime or Dreamland."

"Consciously or not, you get to Dreamland every night," I objected. "It sounds simple and unreal. Can't I be realistic even if I'm just a soul?"

Zar laughed. "Don't you know that even children know the difference between dreams and dreams?" he asked. "Call it dream-knowledge if you like, because it is exactly from those kinds of dreams you get knowledge. They inspire and complete ideas. In this Realm there is a huge cycle of creative dreaming."

"Why not call it the dream-cycle?" I suggested.

"Okay," Zar agreed and continued, "You can look at a cycle as a circle, and the circle is the home-sign for Origin. Our Cosmic Map is a circle with circles in it that create a spiral if you lift it in the middle. One of the most important laws in your Universe is the Law of the circle. Everything starts with a circle, and because it has no end and no beginning the circle is the holy sign of eternity."

"Yes, that's also what the Indians believe," I admitted.

"They realized this very early on," Zar answered. "Now listen, Jan! We will enter the Dream Cycle, so that you understand how it works. There are outer and deeper layers in this Realm, but you ought not to enter the deeper layers alone if you don't know what they contain. I mean that it is important that you feel Oneness with all Creation. You are not alone or abandoned. You are one with All and with Love, and nothing evil can befall you in our Worlds. You have to be aware of that as you enter the Dream Cycle. You need to know that a knowledge awaits you there: a knowledge based upon your inner feeling of wholeness or detachment. Whatever happens, hold on to the wholeness!"

It was a dizzying journey into the Dream Cycle. We all three sailed hand in hand, borne aloft on some kind of airwave. I was not afraid. Why should I be, when I was already dead and buried? Yet I never felt more alive than now! This fantastic life with its marvelous richness of everything, absolutely everything, and more than you can imagine – a life with no room for fear. Terror, fright, and worry are Earthly feelings that do not belong to these nonphysical physical worlds. It is not easy to explain all this. I feel physical, except that some Earthly unpleasant needs have disappeared. I feel free, happy, and rich. On Earth I was a poor devil – here I'm rich!

Mountains, cliffs – are there more words to describe these fantastic creations that as clear as glass raised their glittering tops beneath us? There were snow-capped peaks and now and then we caught a glimpse of azure-blue mountain lakes like sapphires, set in the golden crown of the mountains. We flew over all this at such high speed that I could only perceive a fraction of it. It was more magnificent than on Earth – it was grand! At the same time I realized that this was a landscape where anything could happen. Everything we saw was wrapped in an inexplicable magic. Here fantasy met fairy tale and fairy tale met reality. There are really no words for it!

Below we could discern villages, castles, and simple timber-cottages, but there was no time to see any details. At last we descended and landed in the center of a small village, surrounded by snow-covered mountains. It looked just like Tyrol. The houses, though, were different. They were in bold colors and had beautiful paintings along the sides and gables.

"Is there a Tyrol here too?" I merrily asked. "Will I soon see men in green feather-trimmed hats and leather shorts playing the accordion?"

"I don't think so," Zar answered unsmilingly. "We are going on a boat-tour now."

There was a little lake at the end of the village. We got into a rowboat that was tied to a landing stage. I didn't see any people. The boat started of its own accord. On the other side of the lake there was a high mountain, and a magnificent waterfall poured down its shimmering cascades into the water below, where it made giant foaming waves. We went straight towards the waterfall. I didn't like it; I grasped the sides of the boat tightly.

Shala laughed at me. "You're still unnecessarily afraid for your body," she mocked. "I wouldn't have believed it! You must be wondering why there are no people here. This is a prototype of a landscape that is used in the Dream Cycle. We are not the ones who populate the region or fill it with incidents; that is what dreams do! Those who dream that they come here may get lost in the mountains, fall into the waterfall, fight in the pub, or make love among the rhododendron bushes in the parson's garden. Everybody sees this landscape in a different way, depending on their own capacity for dreaming."

"I must interrupt you," I cried. "Are visions the same thing as the Dream Cycle, or a part of it?"

"A vision is an image which comes to a human being in order to bring him enlightenment or give him pause for thought. A vision isn't derived from the Dream Cycle, but may sometimes be a part of it. You see a vision as a kind of image, short-lived or long-lived, close to or far off. It means that you must help somebody or realize something. The vision comes from your Inner Self. It is created by the unconscious mind with a conscious goal. In contrast, the landscapes of the Dream Cycle are all prototypes. There are infinite numbers of them, which are then recreated or populated by the dreamer. The dreamer creates his own experiences in the landscape. If he wants, he can see the whole landscape or only fragments of it. He directs his part in the Dream Cycle with or without a guide – both things are possible."

I sighed. Did I understand any of this?

"Yes, it is incomprehensible," Shala added with a smile. As usual, she read my thoughts. "You have to have been there and struggled with it. It is a fairy tale world with dragons, witches, and knights. The princess with long golden curls sits in her tower waiting, the hare and the wolf walk together, and Little Red Riding Hood is dancing the jitterbug with the three little pigs. If you want a fairy tale – make one up! If you want a lesson on something, ask for it. If you want to take a walk in the forest and see goblins, fairies, and other Nature Spirits go by, you can do that! You get what you desire. If you want to travel to another country and see something special, you will be able to. The Dream Cycle is the land of possibilities, a land where anything can happen – and I mean *anything!* Sometimes the Indians use the Dream Cycle to see into the future. There are no constants, only a chimera of beautiful variants, delights for eye and mind. Now hurry up, dear, we must leave!"

She had hardly finished saying this when we were whirled away in a rose-colored fog. Of course, I thought, the Realms of Dreams must be rose-colored. But what are we doing here? Dreams couldn't belong to this existence. I was no longer on Earth, where there were both day-dreams and night-dreams. What could I possibly learn here?

"A lot!" was the calm answer from Zar. "The Realms of Dreams are versatile. You have come here to learn how dreams are constructed. Remember, Jan, you are at school!"

The rose-colored fog disappeared and we were standing outside an old castle like the one along the shores of the river Rhein. There was a bustling throng in the courtyard. There were knights on horses and standard-bearers walking around. There were squires, stamping, and noise. In the middle of it all was a fair. There were probably a hundred multicolored stalls with gaudy goods.

"Am I in a Medieval incarnation?" I asked.

"No," Shala answered "You're right in the middle of somebody's dream! There are lots of different dreams in this Realm. They don't last long – look!"

I became interested in a tournament that was starting at the far end of the courtyard and I started to run towards it. As I did so, it all disappeared and I was running on a wet beach with a stormy sea on one side and high sand dunes on the other. I bent down and picked up a shell, and in it was a wonderful pearl. But it all disappeared – again.

"These are normal, muddled dreams," Shala told me. "We call them 'rainbow-dreams,' and there are plenty of them. There are also almost physical dreams and nightmares. The latter are generally caused by the subconscious experiences of the dreamer and are controlled by our main enemy: fear. Day-dreams appear now and then, often bringing light, because they are mostly based on longing. Never despise dreams; each one of them has a meaning."

"If you remember them," I added and stopped. We had been walking slowly, and now we were standing on a path which wound its way into the distance as far as the eye could see.

"You chose this path," Shala said mischievously. "You are walking towards an unknown goal and you have no chance to run away, either to the right or to the left."

"Oh dear!" I exclaimed. "Do you know if there's a nice pub at the end of the path? A cold beer would go down well!"

"I think that the Realms of Dreams have served their purpose!" Shala smiled. "The next Realm is the unknown goal, but first I want you to meet a man who knows more about dreams than I do. His name is Aurus."

Suddenly there was a tall, vigorous man standing in front of me. His snow-white hair reached his knees and his face seemed chiseled from marble. He was dressed in a pastel-colored coat and held a blooming staff in his hand.

"I'm in charge of the Realms of Dreams," he said in a friendly voice. "Dreams are like naughty children. Difficult to organize. The dreamer lacks any sense of order, and so his dreams may be chaotic while he's sleeping. Fortunately, he seldom remembers anything when he awakens, but he can be very tired from his chaotic dreams. I'm sorry we can't do anything about it from here; it must come from the man himself. An orderly way of thinking brings ordered dreams."

"It sounds boring," I interposed. "My thoughts were never very orderly, so I guess my dreams were never respectable. I probably dreamed of the forbidden fruit both day and night on Earth."

"But you made words out of it," Aurus nodded. "Most artists dream about beauty, even if they don't show it in their works. Dreams play wild games inside the dreamer. But there are other dreams too, and we call these perceptions. They're messages to the dreamer. We want them to be remembered or to be stored in the subconscious mind until they need to make themselves known. They can be warnings, premonitions, or images of the future.

"We also have a department for sending urgent messages down to Earth," continued this strange man, "that is also known as premonition or materialization. Some of these experiences do not occur outside the dreamer nor appear during sleep. They come to the receiver via his brain and are very important to him, and perhaps also to others who might be involved in them. This kind of "wireless telegraphy" will be more and more common in the future. People call it channeling, revelation, or vision. To us it is simply messages and guidance. This kind of manifestation must be clear and strong, but there are times when the medium/receiver doesn't listen carefully enough inwards, and involves his/her own thoughts and ideas in our text. I think Zar has already told you that. Let's go on!"

In a jiffy we were all three in the water. But instead of falling to the bottom of the lake again, we were floating among the clouds. It was really crowded up there. I discovered that the clouds were not clouds, but veils floating by. The veils were dreams on their way to the Dream Circuit. Inside them were sleeping souls.

"Now it's time to leave the Dream Circuit," Zar decided. "It's not a good idea to stay there too long, because you may forget reality in all this wishful thinking and wish-creation."

"Reality?" I asked. "What are you calling reality?"

"True reality is in your heart, in the knowledge of what is right for you and no one else." Zar answered. "When you lived on Earth, that was your reality. Now that you have crossed the border, life here is your new reality. The right reality is inside you, in your feelings, in your thoughts, in your perception, but also in your inner wishes and expectations. You can create a false reality if that is what you want – like the Midsummer-pole, for instance. It won't make you happier. You will know with your whole self when you are living in your entirety."

"I never felt as much alive as I do here," I answered seriously. "Possibly when I was writing, because then I was wholly and totally happy. But afterwards it was the same old rubbish."

"You are still writing," Shala reminded me sweetly. She put her little hand on my arm. Her light touch was like a spark of life and powerful, living joy.

"You're right," I said, smiling, "and I'm going to carry on with that! Well, then, I must confess that everything is perfect!"

The Realm of Music

While we were talking, we had landed somewhere new. The air was filled with music, and in front of us was a tall, snow-white building with splendidly-adorned pillars, towers, and pinnacles made of gold, and a giant dome-shaped roof that was transparent. We could hear the most beautiful music issuing from it, and took it for a concert hall.

"All music that has been created exists in that building," Shala told me. "Music is distributed from here to other planets and worlds. The first tone which rang out in our Universe, and helped to create it, remains in this building and echoes in all existing music on Earth and other celestial bodies. Music that is polluted with discordant sounds is a musical contamination in the ether that may harm its audience. It irritates people, because it affects the cells in your brain by negatively stimulating certain places. This may result in violence. There are, as you all know, computer-viruses, and there are also music-viruses. A lot of synthetic music is created on Earth, equally synthetic in its structure as in the instruments. We don't have it here. You create from ready-made creations, you see?"

"What do you mean?" I asked. "Do you mean that you recreate existing music with negative tone creations?"

"You can do it if you have the right tools," Shala answered. "We don't do it here; it only takes place on Earth. There are celestial bodies with no music, but the tone is always there and they decide if they want to create something out of it."

"Is this Realm of Music stable and permanent?" I asked. "I mean, how does it really work?"

"Yes," Zar answered. "In contrast to the Dream Circuit, it is totally stable. In the Dream Circuit everything can be dissolved. It is like a world of shadows, a world of color chimera, where everything is permitted without order or duration. The Realm where you are now is, in its way, as 'physical' as Earth. You humans put other sets of values on the physical. You call it non-physical, metaphysical, or spiritual, sometimes religious, when you don't understand it.

"Really, Jan, it's a question of perception. On Earth it is very densely developed, but here it has a more subtle frequency."

I listened. The music penetrated me, filled me with a whirl of sacred tones: tones that glowed, that ached in my heart, and at the same time caressed away all pain and worry. There were tones I recognized and tones I'd never heard before or knew existed. They exploded into such an amazing beauty that flames were burning in my body, and my head was transformed into a thousand white swans sailing around an egg of gold dust. I existed in that egg – my real Self, the Self that is Spirit, the Self that can cry joy, the Self that belongs to Eternity.

I don't know if we were inside the Music Palace. My consciousness was erased and I *was* the music, lived in it, danced with it, and sang with it. But I was dragged from this hardly pragmatic state by Shala, who took my hand and pulled me with her. We were in a new World before I had time to think.

The Nature World

"You've had enough of music," Shala joked. "You need a big kick to wake you up!"

The kick was something she put into my mouth – it might have been vitamin C, because it tasted good and immediately left me as fit as a fiddle. But I don't know if vitamin C is part of the Spirit World. Maybe there are miracle pills there?

"Call it what you like!" Shala tittered. "It was a pill that contains compressed energy in the form of rays that go directly into your brain cells. They are edifying and totally harmless, but of course, pure and healing thoughts are enough. Music has a bewitching influence on many and it may be difficult to get out of the enchantment. Now to something completely different!"

First I could smell something. I looked around. Again we stood near a waterfall, but I had never seen such floral splendor anywhere. Trees, bushes, the ground – everything was dazzling. There was that special odor of moisture, soil, and greenery that comes after rain, but it was more intense and aromatic than on Earth.

"We were so near to the Nature World that I had to make an excursion into it, even if we have far more Realms to visit in the Astral World," Shala confessed. "The Nature Spirits live here. We have come to a small part of a giant landscape."

She stroked my eyes and at once I saw creatures swarming around us. They looked exactly like my own picture of these lovely beings: Every line was exquisite; they were ethereal, swift, and graceful. I also saw what we call goblins, dressed in gray woolen jackets, looking very active, running around with various tools in their hands.

"When a tree dies, its deva comes here," Shala went on. "The spiritual form of the tree comes, too, and settles down here. In this World you'll find all kinds of plants from Earth, as well as flora from other planets. There are many Realms in this World, too, but we're restricting our visit to the Nature Spirits of Earth. I am not sure what you would think of some other beings. They don't resemble ours and might even frighten you.

"Many thousands of years ago, Nature Spirits co-operated with the humans on Earth. You should remember that. You were there from the beginning, and on Zio this was quite natural. Its flora was something absolutely unique, something you cannot find anywhere any more. Nowadays people have lost the ability to talk to Nature Spirits, but it will return when the Earth changes."

"Do you really think there will be great changes? People's minds are too poisoned to understand what they are doing."

"Maybe now. But are you aware of what happens to all these fragile Nature Spirits because of the pollution on Earth?"

"They move back here, don't they?"

"Yes, gradually. But not all of them. Many of them will be so badly hurt that they will have to return to their first energy-state. They must start all over again. Some of them cannot even handle that; they dissolve in pain before returning to a state of pure energy."

"Can that happen to people as well?" I asked in terror.

"No." Shala smiled. "It's not that simple. Humans themselves must pay for what they're doing to Nature, by suffering disease or other problems. When they come here they realize their wrongs. If they don't understand what they have done, they have to wander about in No Man's World or return to Earth immediately, to put right their wrongs."

"The grass under our feet, the flowers we pick and throw away, the branches we pull off, and all other destruction – what happens to the Nature Spirits? And what happens in forest fires?" I asked.

"Fire is a cleansing process," Shala explained patiently. "The seed and the astral image remain and can be recreated. New growth is created under the same conditions. When you tread on grass you must know that not every blade has a Nature Spirit. There is instead a group-deva for every species. That's how it works for small species, even in the Realm of Animals."

"How come the Nature World is so big that it has a circle of its own on the map?"

"Oh Jan, Nature is the most important thing of all! It's the origin of everything. It contains so many Realms, so many secrets, everything that grows, all development. It needs a lot of space. We made an extra circle for Nature on the map because the Nature Spirits need their own World. They are related to the Angels. Nature is the basis for all existence, physical and astral-ethereal. Mother Earth is the breeding and creating first Mother, not only in the physical world and in our Worlds, but also on other planets. The starry sky is a part of Nature. The clouds, lightning, thunder, the aurora borealis, rain, and storms are part of the unlimited existence of Nature."

She took my arm and I sniffed happily the lovely scent of her long hair, which was tickling my cheek. There were fragrances in these wonderful Worlds: music for your ears, scents for your nose – but perhaps not very much for your stomach!

"Oh yes," Shala laughed. "If you want to eat, help yourself! You can create with your thought, can't you? Some children on Earth know that already. They often visit this part of the Nature World and experience their own fairy tales. To them this adventure is quite physical; they have the gift of vivid realization. But grown-ups don't believe them. Now, have a look, Jan!"

We were walking along a wooded path in a real fantasy forest, like an old Swedish forest from earlier years when there were many kinds of trees, not only pines. Mossy mountains, green tussocks with pale, rose-colored linnaea (twinflower) winding its arms around the lingonberry plants, and dense thickets of woodbine and guelder rose lurked between the trees. Our mossy path was full of ants. I could stay here for ages with my beautiful companion.

"Oh no!" Tittering, she caught my thoughts. "We will only be here a short while, so please appreciate your surroundings!"

I turned around, a little embarrassed. The terrible thing was, my Earthly thoughts still haunted my ethereal brain and Shala easily read them. Behind me I discovered a crowd of goblins and other small beings. They stood in a circle watching a small urchin doing funny somersaults that made them all laugh. When I looked up at the treetops I saw thin, beautiful beings flit along from them. They must be tree-devas.

"Yes, that's right," confirmed Shala, and she gave me a mischievous look. "Stop sniffing at my hair and look in front of you!"

In the middle of a meadow ran a brook. In the middle of the brook Neckan was sitting, playing his violin unceasingly. Elves danced around him. Malignant elves came up from roots and black holes in the ground. Far away a giant was walking around in huge, coarse boots. I had never before imagined how it was to live in a real fairy tale.

"You are not in a fairy tale!" Shala laughed her silvery laugh. "I'm showing you all this because you must understand the relationship between the Realms of Nature and fairy tales. They belong together. All these beings live in Nature on a frequency that is invisible for human beings. Do you remember your first incarnations on Earth, Jan? Nature was undestroyed at that time and humans were in daily contact with these beings. But rough, mean human thoughts built barriers between them. In the future we hope that the good fellowship between humans and Nature Spirits will return. Now it seems impossible because the humans are destroying their Earth."

I sat down on a stone and put my fingers into the whirling water. It was so nice. I washed my face and I was happy to still have a face, hopefully a good-looking one.

"You look very nice," Shala laughingly assured me.

I had forgotten that we were working with thought-reading. Sometimes it's really annoying! I was pondering over where the Realm of the Animals was situated.

"The Realm of Animals from Earth is near to the Nature Spirit's Realm," Shala answered my thought. "We'll go there soon. It is the Realm of Animals from Earth, because there are other planets that have animals. The same goes for plants. There are totally different species, but they also have their place in the great Whole. Even the tiniest plant or animal on Earth is represented here by a mother-plant or deva."

"I see flowers in abundance here," I commented, "but I haven't seen how all these Nature Spirits live yet."

"I can't show you that." Shala smiled. "It's impossible, because every little being has its own way of living in symbiosis with its plant."

"How come there are hybrids, then?"

"They also originate here. Nothing is developed in the human brain. Inspiration must come from somewhere. There's a seed, isn't there? Suddenly something is born through a conscious or unconscious action that causes it to diverge from the original plant. It can be a bird, some wind, something alien in the soil that is sucked by the seed. If we go back to the Dream Circle, we know that ideas arise that are often realized by the dreamer. But sometimes when alien materials are added experimentally it can cause great damage. That is something that unfortunately has started to occur on Earth to a frightening extent."

"Do you mean gene manipulation?" I asked.

"Yes, that's what it's called," Shala answered gloomily. "It's not good at all. It has gone too far with experiments for the sake of profit and power. It's very worrying."

"When people clone humans I think they're trespassing on the Great Spirit's territory, aren't they?"

"Neither animals nor humans should be cloned," Shala stated.

84

"Scientists cannot create souls. Cloned beings have no souls. The soul originates in one place only. There are planets where cloning happens a lot. The mechanical functions work and their brains are highly developed, but none of them have any feelings. Their thinking is limited to certain manipulated channels. They are robots made of flesh and blood …"

"This conversation is going downhill rapidly …"

She swiftly put her hand on my eyes and we went out into space … or space came to us? But when she took her hand away I discovered that we were not floating in space. We were passing over a long bridge without touching it with our feet. It must be the bridge between the Nature World and the Ethereal Worlds, I thought. We were surely traveling at the speed of thought.

"Oh no!" laughed the voice of my companion. "We think faster than this, don't we? Look instead at one of our most beautiful bridges. It stretches across the Parallel Worlds and the Incarnation Worlds, which you are not going to visit now."

Light rainbow-colored, glittering clouds were dancing on both sides of the bridge. All the way across the bridge were sculptures, ornaments, and mosaic, and it was really beautiful. We'd slowed down now and I had time to think.

The bridge between now and then, I thought. The bridge between then and beyond. The bridge between dimensions, I decided, because dimension is a measure of extent. We've come from one extent and are on our way to another, my happy thought continued. In algebra the word dimension means degree. But here you cannot graduate our existence in the same way so that one-dimensional straight lines through movement can become two-dimensional planes, and these in turn through further movement can become three-dimensional spaces. Euclid talked about rooms with three dimensions, but he was only a human. I am now in the fourth dimension – that's how it is.

"Don't try to explain what you are experiencing now in human physics!" was Shala's naughty commentary to my thoughts. "You'll have other things to think about when we get over this bridge – and we will, very soon."

The Realm of Animals

It is not easy to talk when you are whizzing around like this, but as we landed on a sandy plain I had to ask, "I can't forget all the information I got on Earth about 'the Astral Plane,' as it is called there, with all its dark mystery, black magic, and low-level sorcery. Ghosts and more or less evil forces, as well as UFOs, are assigned to the Astral Plane. So far I've only seen beautiful, happy, comprehensive, and informative parts of what here is called the Astral World. Where do you keep the frightening and uncanny things? Where are the scoundrels, the 'physically spiritual' people, who earn money by telling they have channels to you?"

"We don't like to talk about the dark side," Zar answered. "It does not exist in the Astral World. It is near to Earth, as you can see on the Cosmic Map, because it has a close relationship to the humans who developed it. The Dark Realms are not the same thing as hell, because Gehenna is to be found on Earth, inside people. Your insufficient religions have created expressions like 'hell,' 'devil,' and 'purgatory.' You don't have any religion which does not mention sin and punishment. The Dark Realms deal with desperation rather than magic, because the black magic that they spread never reaches our Worlds. It ends up in people who are receptive to evil. Does the word 'astra' mean something to you, Jan?"

"It means 'stars' in Latin, doesn't it?" I answered, a little surprised.

"Exactly!" Zar seemed content. "'Astrum' means 'star' and 'astralis' means 'glittering like a star.' Can you connect these words with evil? The beautiful and glittering significance of the word astral has disappeared because of humans. They have changed it into something dark and scary, which originates from the fear and agony that they, themselves, feel. Here you will learn what the Astral World really means – and that is the real astral, the star-glittering one."

"What about the mental level?" I asked. "I have read many books about the mental level, and they say it is one step further than the astral one."

86

"Dear Jan," Zar answered, "the mental level is what exists in your brain and what is not said with your mouth; in fact, your thoughts. Your books are wrong. The mental world is nearer than No Man's World, because it means that your living brains are working. A separate mental world or level doesn't exist. All thinking is mental. You'll find it here too, where it works in a telepathic way. Telepathy is not yet common on Earth, and that's why humans have given mental thought its own level. They use their own terminology, but here we work according to our own language. We want to make the different Worlds understandable for readers, and that is why we cannot use the usual religious terms."

"Have you been looking around?" The soft voice of Shala interrupted us.

I had not. Zar was really turning my well-established preconceptions upside down, but this had been the case since I came here. I realized that everything was much simpler than you could possibly imagine on Earth, and I felt a little ashamed of my ignorance of the Astral. From now on the Astral World would be "the World of the Stars." I looked around happily and on one side of us I saw huge cliffs and on the other side forests. The sandy plain ran down to a lake. I saw wild animals grazing, running around, or resting. It was strange that all these different animals were together; everything from tigers, lions, elephants, zebras, and deer to all kinds of small animals. On Earth we say, "Eat or be eaten." Here I saw a peaceful gathering in fellowship.

"Noah's Ark!" I exclaimed. "All those animals seem to enjoy being together."

"Of course," Shala answered. "Here you find a great variation of scenery for wild animals. We also have a beautiful park with pleasant houses for pets. Each breed, small or large, has its own deva, and these devas nurse their animals. When animals come here they must go through a health check. Not only people believe that they take their diseases with them when they die. Some animals believe they are badly crippled, and they search for lost body parts. Special devas work with these poor animals who have, among other sufferings, been victims of vivisection. How can humans be so cruel as to use animals for their experiments? When are humans going to learn to use healing? Healing can also be used on animals. The communication between humans and animals has also disappeared."

I protested, "Not between dogs, horses, cats, and their owners. I know many very good examples. I wonder if a deeply loved dog, who suddenly dies, may be born again and come back to its former owner?"

"Well, it may vary from case to case. We have animals who refuse to go back to Earth. The animals spread over the map as they like – it is difficult to keep them in their own Realm. Pets, especially horses, dogs, and cats, can be tightly bound to their former owners. We often have reunions between human and animal souls. A human soul who has crossed the border is permitted to have his or her pet in company. Sometimes pets appear as ghosts. I mean that their energies are so strong that they can materialize for a very short moment. But the same goes for animals as for people: They must be given the chance to develop at higher levels. Maybe a dog is not reincarnated as a dog, a cat not as a cat, and so on."

"What happens to them?" I was curious. "Will they be humans?"

"I don't think you need to know any more about this Realm," Zar said. He took my arm again. "Your question needs to be answered on an individual basis. Remember that here, in the Realm of Animals, there is Love between all species of animals. Love permeates all our Worlds, because from the very Beginning we were created from Love."

"I would like to ask a question before we leave. It is a question about the gods of the American Indians. I have heard that different tribes have different names for their gods. Do they mean the same god? The Wampanoag tribe calls the Great Spirit Kiehtan or Kishtannit, and there are lots of other gods beneath him. In North America alone there were more than 500 Indian tribes. That adds up to a lot of different gods, doesn't it? That's only one example; the whole Earth is full of idols. What are you doing about it?"

"An easy question!" Zar was smiling. "Look at the Cosmic Map! Outside No Man's World there are, for example, the Realms of Idols. The gods live there in perfect well-being. If hundreds of tribes in thousands of places on Earth give different names to their gods, it is only a question of language. The gods living in the Realms of Idols each have one original name. The Great Spirit rules them too. We can call the idols symbols, living their own lives. They are far too numerous to be described in detail. Are you ready for the Children's Realm?"

The Children's Realm

Jolith appeared like a giant bird from the clouds above us. She carried us further on her strong wings. We landed in a large play park.

There were swings everywhere, slender silvery swings where children were helped to swing towards the sky – children with fluttering hair, rosy cheeks, and happy eyes. Nobody seemed scared. Laughter lurked and peeped in all small mouths before letting loose. It blared out in happy drumrolls until it choked. Children's voices and joyful screams echoed everywhere. They skipped, played hopscotch, and threw balls. They danced, sang, and listened to fairy tales. I felt bewitched. If there is a Paradise, this is it! Angels glided around, bringing consolation, praise, and encouragement.

I have always been fascinated by fairy tales, even if I didn't give them much of my time. I admit that I was always dreaming of writing children's books, but I never dared to compete with other story-tellers when I was already a well-known novelist. I was also a bit old-fashioned. I loved knights and dragons, captured princesses, trolls in dark forests, and poor little children wandering barefoot across the meadow (as I once had), dreaming of good food. Can modern children relate to that?

"It's delightful here!" I inhaled the scent of a thousand flowers. I could see a small lake where children were bathing, full of noise and splashing.

"It's nice here for the kids," Shala agreed. "Children never come to No Man's World; they are taken directly to the Realm of Children. For a while they live in our gardens for children, retaining the same age and appearance they had at the time of transition. This is necessary for their sense of security. They have to be children yet a while, happy children who laugh and play. But most of them have to return to Earth. Before that, they go to a school nearby. They have to choose new parents and understand their choice in order to be able to meet the future on their own volition."

"The poor children who are born on Earth today," I sighed. "Some of them become child laborers and soldiers from the age of eight, in developing countries. Some of them are born to parents who will soon divorce, with all that that entails. I wonder how many of them will have a good and happy life on Earth."

"There we have the Power of thinking again," Shala explained. "If they succeed in bringing the right sort of thinking with them, and can listen inwardly and act in accordance with what they hear, they will not be unhappy. But things may go wrong if they succumb to the pressure of their surroundings.

"When the next step is ready for a child, he or she is moved to another part of the Children's Realm. I can't tell you how, but a metamorphosis takes place there, resulting in a change of age for the child. Well, it's difficult to use the word age in this context, because age doesn't exist here. Mostly the soul has undertaken a short previous lifetime for karmic reasons. This may have to do with the family or with victims, especially when it comes to group reincarnations in developing countries where mass murder and mass exodus take place.

"Today we allow the kids to carry thoughts from us in their subconscious minds. Many children born today are spiritually developed. They have been gifted with a spiritual seed, but it needs nourishment in order to grow."

"Children who die early, especially those who die in terrible circumstances – war, starvation, murder – did they choose to be born on Earth for a few years in order to experience all those awful things?" I wondered, realistically.

"Mostly they did," was the answer. "There are accidents, but nothing is coincidental. Death works like this: Most people have a number of posts or stop signals on their road through life. It is not predestined that you will die at a certain time. There are several possibilities or accidents to end a life. It is in fact you, or rather your Higher Self, that decides when it's time. Your Higher Self knows this better than you. It can see what is happening in your deepest soul and what needs an extension of your life to develop. You do not realize, but the decision is yours! You can survive a difficult operation, a car accident, a drowning accident, or something else that challenges death. Why? Because you are not finished with the life you have chosen for yourself, while other people think that a miracle saved you."

"Is that also relevant in the case of heart transplants?"

"That depends. In our eyes, we regard playing with divine forces as unnatural. Whatever the doctors say, healing could have been as good as transplantation – but you haven't got that far yet. A lot depends on the will of the patient to survive. The result of transplantation might be negative, because the patient is getting not only a new organ, but also the energies of that organ. But that's another story."

"Many people who have just started their career on Earth are taken away much too early," I objected, "and that goes for children too."

"You are using the wrong expressions!" cried Shala. "Career! Do you know where that career could have taken that person if he'd lived? Be taken away – how silly! Nobody is taken away; everybody is passing through. The family might feel its member has been taken away, and they may snatch at him so that he has difficulty crossing No Man's World."

"You just talked about accidents. Do they exist?"

"Difficult question. Accidents occur because of people's negligence, sloppiness, or thoughtlessness," Zar answered seriously. "They depend on the creation of negative thoughts, a kind of landslide in the subconscious that leads to carelessness in the conscious mind."

"Most children who come here are much happier here than they were on Earth," Shala eagerly assured me. "They get the chance of a new life which can be much better, because here they learn to understand everything they didn't understand before. They take that knowledge with them in their subconscious mind, and if they listen to their intuition they will be given a new chance. No child dies without a cause. Nothing is left to chance. The reason for an early death, which is clearly expressed from here, may naturally be obscured by their Earthly surroundings. The family mourns and they may blame themselves – but it is their karma. You have seen singing, dancing, play, and joy – free and happy children in a world where words like bullying or violence are totally unknown. Here a child might get hurt, but they don't experience pain. They never hit each other and are never beaten. Do you understand? Let's go on."

I saw children and Nature Spirits playing together. The Nature World and the Children's Realm were in close contact with each other. Goblins and elves, which were only fairy tales on Earth, existed here. There is a Realm called Fairy Tale Realm in the Astral World, next to the Children's Realm. Giants and trolls live there and fairy tales, myths, and adventures take place all the time. Sometimes the Angels must interfere in order to bring order in these wild fairy tales.

"Sometimes," Shala said with a laugh, "bold kids can visit the Fairy Tale Realm and experience fantastic adventures. No harm can touch them, even if they have a tough time, because as soon as they are afraid, the fairy tale dissolves and they return here. I wish more adults would remain young at heart and visit this Realm. To be child-like is good for human beings. Would you like to stay here for a while, Jan?"

"Thank you," I very swiftly answered, "but I'm inquisitive and would like to go on."

Suddenly Jolith appeared and rushed off all three of us.

"You asked a question a while ago that I haven't answered yet," Zar said while we were traveling. "You wonder where the spirit rogues live. Many of them inspire and guide psychics over the whole world. They are clever, inventive tricksters from No Man's World who really believe that they *are* who they claim to be. They borrow names from the Bible and other religious books. Some of what they say is really true and they are well informed by forces which do not belong to our worlds. Some of them are pulling their victims' legs, and yet others have a plan behind their supposed channeling, a plan which didn't originate here."

"How can you tell the difference?" I asked. "How can you know who's who? How can a psychic trust his or her own intuition if there are such forces in circulation?"

"My dear friend, intuition is the greatest Master. But as I've told you before and as you already know, there are many inhabited planets in our galaxy, and some of them want to usurp power on Earth – like Orion, which we've already mentioned. They send a lot of 'psychic' information."

"But that's terrible," I cried. "Who can trust whom?"

"When you turn to your Inner and Higher Self and ask, you will always get the right answer."

"I might think that I'm doing just that and get the answer wrong anyway." I was a little angry. "People on Earth don't have the same resources as you have here."

"You will know what comes from your Inner Self and what is right," Zar assured me, "and you'll see the result. Don't forget that your ego may want to participate. When inspiration is egotistical, the result may be wrong."

"Oh," I sighed, "you make me so confused."

"Not at all," said the mild voice of Shala. "Zar means that when money and power are involved, you have to be careful. Knowledge from a channel must emanate out of Love without any demands for payment. That's the secret in a nutshell!"

"There won't be many honest psychics left, in that case," I sighed. "Poor good old Earth that is sown with so many weeds!"

"Dear Jan," Zar said in a serious voice. "This isn't about beautiful words, but about the way you apply them. Anyone can talk about light, but not everyone *is* light or can *bring* light. The reason for good, loving words must not be profit. These two polarities displace each other and force on unwanted goals. Let people visit different psychics to receive varying information. That is one way to learn. You have to make mistakes in order to understand what's good or bad. There are many good psychics. I should just warn you that sensitive people may be influenced by some planets. Now we are landing!"

94

9. The Midnight Mass

"I haven't seen any churches yet," I remarked, as the Angel's wings spread its soft feathers on the ground like a sail.

"There are no churches in our Worlds," Zar answered. "Why would we need churches? We sent down our Brother, Jesus Christ Sananda, to Earth. His mission was to tell humans that All is One. Your religions divide instead of unite. Churches are temples of power for priests. Why don't you use churches for playing beautiful music and songs in, and let people go into them to pray without anyone taking a collection in the name of God? – a collection that is not always conducted positively, by the way."

"Are you talking about God in the Old Testament?" I asked.

"Of course. You won't see any churches here, unless it's a hologram church in No Man's World. But holograms disappear quickly. We have real buildings here where we meet, sing, dance, and send light."

"Wouldn't a Midnight Mass be charming?" I ventured.

"Yes, you will experience a charming Midnight Mass before we leave this place. Then you'll stop talking about churches. Now look around!"

It seemed as if we were standing on an airfield, but the runways were different from those on Earth, though many colored lights were blinking everywhere. Shala beckoned me to come, and we entered a giant, silvery building, reminiscent of an observatory. In the middle of it was a spiral staircase. When we were up near the top, we found a landing with a rail that ran around the whole building. The walls were very thin and transparent; you could imagine you were standing outside. The sky was an indigo color and the stars seemed so near that you could almost touch them. From our elevated position we saw a gigantic platform where ships were landing. Some of them looked like flying saucers, others like Zeppelins, and yet others were impossible to describe.

95

"We are still in the Astral World," Zar explained, "and this is a landing-place for visitors from outer Space. There are planets whose inhabitants can adjust themselves to our frequency without crossing the boundary of physical death."

"Is this a Realm in the Astral World?" I asked.

"No," Zar answered, "this is nothing more than an airbase. There are buildings here where Angels take care of the visitors and tell them where to go. You mentioned Realms, and I must tell you that not far from here is the Main Database for all the Worlds, as it might be called in Earthly language. It so huge that it contains every living and non-living soul on Earth. We will not show this database, since it is so enormous and complicated, that the uninitiated can't possibly understand how it works. For example, there you can find all the lives one single person has lived since the first time he was born as a human. Without it we couldn't have shown you your Akashic Record. This technical area belongs to the Scientific Realm."

"Thanks! I'm no technician, so that's no place for me. I prefer the Realm of Beautiful Arts."

"Good, because that's our next port of call," Zar told us.

"Why did you show me this airbase?" I asked.

"Because it is a border area and because we are going to fly again," Shala answered. "You wanted to experience a Midnight Mass and we invite you one – without a church."

Something that looked like a glass ball landed behind us. We climbed into the craft and sat down. It was very much like a helicopter, but everything was made of glass – even the chairs. What I here call glass was a transparent material which didn't feel hard when you touched it. The chairs molded themselves to our bodies. There was no sign of any pilot. Where Zar sat there was an instrument panel and some levers.

"You're not frightened?" Shala teased me.

I denied it, of course. What had I to be frightened of? What was I expecting? Not a church, but a huge concert hall, on another planet perhaps. Life after death was full of surprises, which suited me down to the ground. I remembered when I was ill with a disease which was incurable at that time. At first, things felt hopeless, but then my resistance kicked in, as high as the Eiffel tower. I didn't want to be ill, wither, and die, just as I had seen happen in other farm laborer families, because of the lack of nutrition, damp houses, heavy work, and other misery. I remember sitting on a stump in the forest, thinking very hard. I realized I had not brought much fun or happiness to my home or elsewhere, but if I lived, I would show them. I made a radical decision on that stump. I was going to *think* myself well.

Strangely enough, I succeeded. This kind of thinking was completely unknown at that time. Maybe I had got something out of an old book – I cannot remember. But my whole life changed when I recovered and stubbornly went from publisher to publisher in order to get my books printed. Thought won through in the end – even if it took its time!

Outside the glass ball was an indigo-blue sky, embroidered with so many glittering star sequins that they almost hurt my eyes. I saw whirling planets and comets – or was it perhaps shooting stars that fizzed by like fire-breathing dragons? The glass ball rolled around in the clear atmosphere, and if we had not been fastened in, our light bodies would have been dissolved in the turbulence. Yet this rolling was not unpleasant, because space provided a thrilling performance whichever way we looked – up, down, or sideways. We were surrounded by the cosmos; we were small atoms in the Wholeness. If we screamed, our voices would make less noise than the fluttering of a butterfly wing. But we couldn't scream; our lips were sealed. Our eyes were seized by the All, and our bodies collected a hitherto unknown energy that gave us high after high of raised consciousness, almost like a primal shock. I felt as if I was about to explode from the inside.

Suddenly it came. Somewhere in the glass ball a hatch opened and sounds could be heard. The Midnight Mass had started. It was the music of space, the overtones of the spheres, the harmonies of the Angels, and the sacred choruses of the Seraphim. The unity of light and sound not only reached our ears, but invaded our whole bodies and stretched our limbs in naked adoration.

We were floating in the biggest place thought can create: space. The tones searched for us – not vice versa. They flew around our ship, playing in circles parading on top of each other. With a sound of fragile crystal the tones were pulled upwards in a spiral, with us in its center. Our nerve fibers were seething. The rushing and singing swept us into a cathedral of sound. It was frighteningly beautiful, but no words can ever explain what we experienced at this eternal moment in the arms of the ether.

Zar, Shala, and I were prostrate in the glass ball, floating in the air. We floated with the tones, and the tones floated into us. There were sounds I had never heard before, streaming over me in cascades as if from a gigantic waterfall. 'All the churches and cathedrals of Earth are nothing compared to this!' I thought. All I have ever read, all the masters of music and art, all the culture of the whole world was nothing compared to this sublime moment. Perhaps my eternity is not the same as yours, dear Earthlings, but right now mine was speaking. The Eternity was telling its story! It was singing of its infinity, its Unconditional Love, and its tremendous beauty. Could the sweetest of all sweet things cause pain? Can pain and happiness be bound together in a feeling so strong that what we call death on Earth is a symphony of joy? And I ask, what actually are *feelings*? I know I have kept my gift *to feel* after crossing over, but never before have I felt that I am made up only of feelings!

Midnight Mass had not finished. Outside the glass ball it suddenly started to burn. I immediately sat up and looked out into the cosmos. Our ship was surrounded by flames that didn't look like burning fire. This was not a fire of hot, burning flames. This was a fire of colors, making patterns, following the rhythm of the tones. It was so beautiful, my euphoric feelings left me stunned. I sat erect, absorbing everything and wishing it would never end. I wanted to remain in this little glass cage out in space, long after Midnight Mass had faded away. How was it possible to return to any existence after this?

The darkness of compassion made me sleep for a short while. When I awoke we had landed at the airbase and Shala helped me out. I was trembling.

"You will get used to our Midnight Masses," she comforted me, as my tears dropped onto her hand. I could still cry.

"You see," she went on in a soft voice, "this was the first time you were with us, but there will be many more times. You have to get in practice for the highest happiness, just as for anything else."

"This must be the greatest thing to happen to any soul, apart from meeting the Divine Father," I panted.

Shala laughed sweetly. "You don't need to meet him separately," she assured me. "He is everywhere and in everything. You have him inside you, and he conducted this great midnight symphony!"

"But I thought he was in the middle of the circles of the Cosmic Map," I stammered. "That's where the Great Spirit, the Father-Mother, lives, isn't it?"

"Oh yes," Shala tittered. "Of course he is there. But he is everywhere as well."

Zar joined us. He gripped my shoulders and gave me a friendly pat on the back. "He is in your muse, he is in your heart, he is in your eyes and in mine and in Shala's," he said. "The All-Seeing Eye is part of your own eye, but that part doesn't always open when you live on Earth.

"And now I'm back to the subject of churches. The priests give people the wrong image of the Father. He is the Highest One. But as he is in all eyes, in all hearts, he cannot be higher up than we are, can he? It's true that he has his Beingness in the middle of our Cosmic Map. But from there he radiates a spark to every living cell. Every living thing contains the energies of the Creator. That's the strongest law that exists.

"And now, Jan, we'll continue our journey."

10. The Realm of Beautiful Arts

The Realm of Beautiful Arts is also a center for creation. From there energy-rays emanate to all art that is created on Earth. I was wondering why some art is so ugly, so base and disgusting – and yet it's called art. Is it really created up here?

"The energies inspiring artists all over the Earth are sent from here," Zar answered. "But in order to reach the artist as inspiration, the aura must be penetrated. The inspiration is only able to teach the artist by way of the aura. If the aura is sick or influenced by evil, drugs, or negative thinking, the inspiration will be transformed on its way to realization by the artist's interpretation of images. Therefore not all art on Earth becomes Heavenly or celestial. Take a look at your own inspiration, Jan!"

I did. I was amazed to see the old farm laborer's cottage where I was born, the cattle I tended, the fields we plowed, the church where all we children were baptized, and the meadows, the forest, and the lakes all around. All of that appeared around me. I was standing in the middle of a holistic center of my own childhood.

"This is where you found power and inspiration," Shala whispered into my ear. "Your simple, uncomplicated childhood gave you strength, even if you often found your life troublesome and insufficient. This landscape inspired your pen to write all those words that were colorful and picturesque. Your words would have been empty and uninteresting, had you not dwelt in these surroundings. That's how it is for most artists. Their childhood and adolescence characterizes them for good or bad. But their hands do not always follow their inner images. Many of them bear stones with them from life to life. Such artists do not belong to The People of the Sun and the Stars – they belong only to their ego."

My native place disappeared, and instead a studio appeared. Several artists were painting there. The paintings were sublime. They were so beautiful and were painted in different styles and on different material. Earthly eyes never saw anything like it.

"This is art which will directly inspire Earth-artists as energies," Zar told us. "We will see what becomes of it when it reaches its terrestrial receivers."

"I can tell you that!" I laughed. "Not one grain of all this beauty will stick to terrestrial canvas. If it really did it would change people and raise their consciousness."

Souls who were artists, or would like to have been, could come here if they wanted to. There are teachers and the possibility of practicing all kinds of art. When you walk around here you often are struck by the familiarity of the paintings on the walls. Famous terrestrial artists, who have not incarnated on Earth again, share their experiences and skills. Less famous artists get a new start.

The surroundings faded and I saw a lot of rooms around me. Everything was included, from a simple garret to a magnificent library. All were authors' workshops. Heaps of books were lying on a big table. Their titles were fantastic, and somehow I knew that these books were perfect. They were the books that had never been written. They were books that would revolutionize the world, that would reverse all prejudice, hammer nails into the gigantic coffins of religions, and pave the way for a new, positive, and different conception of life. There were books for children and grown-ups. Some titles touched on recently-published books that already exist. This was the trend that was awakening on Earth, the thrilling literature of the future.

I wanted to stay here. I rummaged around in the books on the table. It felt so good to handle them, feel their weight or lightness, and drink in whatever caught my eyes. I found no Bible among all these books, but a heavy history-book of religion, with gilt edges and beautiful pictures. I skimmed through to the end. The last page revealed how all religions were about to converge into a single conception of life where only One Source of power ruled through every living individual. I looked questioningly at Shala.

"That book is a vision of the future," she explained in a soft voice. "It shows what we are aiming for."

"Can I stay here for a while?" I asked. "Can you fetch me later on?"

Shala shook her head.

"It won't get you anywhere, it's wasting of our time. This is your personal interest, but your readers wish to continue and learn more. Zar is waiting for us in the Angelic Realm, in the Ethereal World – so, let's go!"

11. The Angelic Realm

Again I experienced clouds or fog. A sheer haze of blue, rose, and violet wrapped itself around us so tightly that I could hardly see the contours of Shala anymore, but I could feel the firm grip of her little hand. It reminded me of the kind of smoke curtains that are used on stage and in movies. I wondered if perhaps I was still the old Jan, who hadn't died, but was dreaming all of this. Reality becomes blurred when you pass through the Realms of Dreams. I doubted my reality and wondered where it could be found.

"You must trust me, Jan!" Shala's voice was very determined. "You have closed your eyes because you do not dare to be who you are now: the man on the other side of the Portal of Light. Look up now, my friend. This is your reality!"

It was really bright. I heard lovely music, and my nose scented the most pleasant fragrances, spicy and aromatic. But shouldn't Angels have wings? At least that is the ancient view on Earth that is portrayed in old books, pictures and churches. Angels *must* have wings!

Here there were figures, dressed in light clothes, walking around in a tremendously beautiful park, a paradise like in a French painting from the eighteenth century. Not one of them had wings. Yet I saw light shining around them, like a halo or an aura.

"It is their radiation," Shala explained with a smile. "You are still thinking in Earth terms. But now you have to wake up and try a new way of thinking. I brought you to this park in order to let you study the Angels in peace. I thought you had understood the question of wings. This is a creative world. If, by any chance you should need wings, you create them."

"The backs of these Angels look too weak to bear wings," I remarked. "You'd need to be very muscular to have them."

"Would you call bumble bees bundles of muscles?" Shala asked with a laugh. "Have you noticed the slim, tender wings that carry their plump, solid bodies? But they work! Your laws of physics are not relevant here, yet you refer to them repeatedly, Jan! Forget the old and make way for the new! You are learning something quite new and wonderful. But you will have to accept magic that is easy for us, even if it is labeled 'sorcery' on Earth. Jolith is living proof of this. She uses our magic so that she can grow and carry us on her strong wings out into space. Now let's continue on our exploring expedition."

You can't talk about towns here. On Earth any largish accumulation of houses is called a town, but here I would prefer to call them meeting-points or focuses. The buildings we saw were schools, concert halls, libraries, and town halls. These buildings are there only for cultural or developmental reasons. Shala and I made a short journey that gave me a summary of most of what is on our Cosmic Map.

I believe the reader is wondering how the Masters and the Angels live and also how all these Worlds are built up. You want to know how the inhabitants live their daily lives, because you must always think in Earthly terms. There is no day and night in these Worlds, but there is rest. Everybody has the right to stillness and rest whenever they want. Since there is neither time here nor subdivision of time in days and hours, we can call our life here an *eternal beingness*." Maybe it sounds dull to your ears, but I can assure you that it is a very thrilling, active, and nice way of beingness.

If you would like to inspect the homes of the Angels you would probably have a tough challenge. Houses for Masters and Angels are those homes that each and every one create for themselves in a rich and changing landscape. Both the Ethereal and Astral Worlds are situated in gigantic nature areas, seemingly without beginning or end. Inside these areas we can create the surroundings we like. When you get tired of the old surrounding, which in many cases resembles the one we had when we left the Earth, it is easy to dissolve it. You can build something new or choose to move from place to place. Big and beautiful establishments, that you could call "hotels," are situated here and there. It is difficult to describe them, but they are a very pleasant kind of collective living, where everybody is welcome and where there is always a comfortable room to stay in as long as you wish. If you want company, there are small and large recreation areas and rooms for meditation. It's difficult to describe more of the Ethereal World, since it is so changeable.

There are lots of Realms in the Astral World; we have talked about the most important ones. You can also say that the Astral World is less ethereal than the Realms of the Angels and Masters. There is another difference too: It is not necessary to be visible in the Ethereal World. It's voluntary and up to the wishes of the individual. To me it's always strange when an invisible soul talks to me. I prefer to be visible and to be with visible friends. Invisible souls appear as rays of light. Sometimes the light takes on a shape and then becomes a person. I can do that too, when it is practical, especially if I have a mission on Earth. The soul always radiates an aura that is more or less pale. If you don't want to be seen, it moves off to the ceiling or to floor level.

I have used the word "school" in various contexts: the Angels' School, the Astral World's Schools, and so on. What I call "school" does not correspond to physical schools on Earth. With "school" I mean a place to find knowledge. The schools in the Astral World develop human souls. If a soul in No Man's World asks for help to come further, it instantly ends up in such a school. The soul will be allowed to grow in the direction it desires, having consulted the helping Angels.

The Angel's School in the Ethereal World has yet another purpose, but I've already told that. It educates and develops those who choose not to incarnate any more, but continue within an area they choose themselves. For instance, there are different Soul Groups that are taught about their collective task and their individual missions, which may involve missions to Earth. The novices in the light city of Shamballa, in the Realms of the Masters, need a lot of time preparing in the Angels' School before they can assimilate the higher education.

Suddenly I was very thirsty. "Is it possible to get something to drink?" I asked Shala, feeling almost ashamed. She laughed.

"Help yourself; we serve both food and drink!" she said. "When we want to eat or drink something, we create it. The character of our food and drink enables them to be absorbed into our ethereal bodies and dissolved without any trace."

She handed me a goblet from nowhere and I drank greedily. It tasted wonderful and was very refreshing.

"I thought you knew this by now," Shala scolded. "You are your own creator and your wishes will be fulfilled within reasonable limits. If we want to walk in beautiful nature, we do so. If we want to move on swiftly, we do so by the power of thought."

I already told you that the 'hospitals' here are for sleeping souls who need information and helping treatment. Many people who die believe that they still are ill, and cannot leave their Earthly problems behind. We have skilled healers. Many of them were doctors on Earth, and they go on helping people here and via mediums on Earth.

There is no particular Realm for the reunion of souls. This may take place in all Worlds. Normally the first questions that are asked when souls arrive here are, "Can I see my wife, husband, mother, father?" etc. Sometimes there are immediate reunions. Sometimes it takes longer – the missing one might have reincarnated. Here the individual soul develops according to its wishes and abilities, fully independent of its last life on Earth. Liberation from relatives has to take place, even if it is difficult. We cannot be dependent on a strongly bound emotional life that is connected with someone other than our own Dual. But I must admit that we often get Romeo and Juliet cases. We allow them to be together for a time until they understand that they are unique souls, each of which must choose its own way. If they belong to the same Soul Group – which happens quite often – they can proceed in the fellowship and All-Love that is there. People who need to solve common problems in order to go further receive help from the Angels. Music is very healing in these cases.

With regard to the Realm of Science, which we just fluttered into and out of very swiftly, it is rather complicated. It is a Realm where ideas are born and where these ideas are tested in practice on an ethereal level. I was never interested in science, but I admired the beautiful public buildings, every one of them an architectonic masterpiece.

The Realm of Science made me ask Shala what the word "religion" means here.

"Religion," she snorted, "is not allowed here! How would it be if every soul prayed to different gods? Here there is just *one* Creator; what would we need with a bundle of religious symbols? Your Christ is working in Shamballa, where he calls himself Sananda. He is also one of the members of the Galactic Council, together with Buddha and other highly developed spirits. We have no churches, no mosques, and no synagogues.

"The word "religio" means to worship God and to gather around him. You can do that under the roof of the grand Universe – there is no need of a particular building!"

The Banquet

"I hope Shala taught you some interesting things," Zar said, embracing me. "We are going to have a banquet in your honor! You will meet the Archangels and the Elohim."

"Isn't that the same thing?" I asked.

"Absolutely not," Zar answered. "The seven Archangels, of whom there are actually nine now, and the seven Elohim have quite different tasks. Follow me to the banquet hall and I will tell you more."

"A banquet in my honor?" I repeated, surprised. "That doesn't sound likely, because I am quite a humble person."

"My little joke." Zar smiled. "In a way it's true. The Angels love to have parties. You are an author who has an assignment to supply news from here, so they decided to organize a party and invite you."

The building – was it a pyramid? It was gigantic and made of what looked like gold and glass. It was built as a pyramid with four small pyramids, one on each side. Until this moment I had considered that the Blue Hall and the Golden Hall in Stockholm's Town Hall were the most beautiful rooms I had ever seen. I now changed my mind. I cannot describe in words something that is never seen on Earth. A verbose author may sometimes be silenced. What I can say is that there were long tables with gold-shimmering table-cloths and high-backed chairs. There were no places laid for dinner, but I didn't feel hungry. I felt satisfied just looking upon all this splendor.

Zar gestured to me to sit down at one of the long sides of the table with him, Shala, and Jolith. When I looked up to the pointed roof far above, I could see no lamps. A soft and wonderful light colored the hall pale rose. Along the walls were double rows of balconies and parapets.

"Listen to me," Zar urged, patting my arm. "You want to know the difference between Elohim and Archangels. Archangels mostly work with Earth. Elohim have their missions all over the Universe – all galaxies, planets, and stars. They administrate our Universe by working with the ruling energies in the Wholeness. The Archangels do the same thing in a more tangible way with the Earth, the Sun, the Moon, and some other planets. Why?

"Well, because from now on the Earth needs special help. It is crucial to save Earth, the atmosphere around it, and the nearest constellations, and to prevent the compressed stream of poison Earth releases into the cosmos from destroying everything that surrounds it. I promise you it is an enormous task they are performing. But there are many of us helping."

"Do the Elohim and Archangels govern these gigantic spaces as helpers to the Great Spirit?" I asked. "Are they the Lords of the world and the Universe?"

"Now you are silly," Zar exclaimed, frowning. "You're thinking in symbols of power again. That's not allowed here. We have no political organizations and no cosmic mafia. Somebody has to organize and administrate, but that has nothing to do with power, only with law and order."

"Oh," I interposed a bit cheekily, "So who writes the laws? Do you perhaps have some kind of Cosmic Tribunal here? Law and order sounds so damn legal."

"You have seen your origin," Zar answered patiently. "You wouldn't be sitting here at my side if you had not been *created* from the beginning. Who created you, a tiny spark in the cosmos?"

"The Great Spirit, of course!" I felt rather confused.

"Could you possibly imagine that He, when He created his Universe, had to do it with law and order? Somewhere something has to prevent chaos, and that has nothing to do with either power or judicial law."

"But after that," I insisted, "all the other old men were created. Wasn't there already a risk of discrimination?"

Zar gave a hearty laugh, and so did Shala and Jolith. I couldn't see the funny side of it. I was trying to understand the meaning of law and order in the Universe. It is not easy when you still have some Earthly pieces still left inside your ethereal head. I leaned over to Zar.

"Listen," I said in a low voice, "I heard a couple of friends talking about meetings with Angels. One of them talked about wings, the other two claimed that the Angels looked like ordinary humans. One of my friends was rescued out of a car that collided with a wall of rock on a slippery, deserted road. A man, who looked completely ordinary, pulled him out of the car before it exploded. When it did explode, my friend was already well away from the car. Yet he knew that the collision and the explosion happened simultaneously. How did the stranger get him out of the car? At first my friend thought he was a lumberjack, but the stranger was dressed in a neat dark coat and a felt hat. One moment the rescuer was behind my friend right in the middle of the explosion – the next moment he had totally disappeared and the burning car was 20 meters away. There was only one explanation: The rescuer was an Angel."

"I just told you that Angels are good at all kinds of white magic," Zar said. "In the case of an emergency situation, Angels often take on the shape of a human being, because they don't want to frighten the victim. Look here!"

A young boy dressed in a white shirt and light brown trousers came up to us and greeted me in a friendly way. He brought with him a girl in jeans and a flowery blouse. The boy was blond-haired and looked Scandinavian. The girl had red hair, freckles, and mischievous blue eyes.

They looked completely terrestrial. Were they newcomers in this World?

I barely had time to finish thinking before the youngsters changed into beings wearing light, pastel-colored clothes like the ones I wore. I was astonished. From their thin backs I saw enormous white wings emerge. I had heard such things could happen, but I'd never seen it before. Magicians on Earth would have been green with envy seeing this!

"A little performance, just for you!" Shala laughed. "Sometimes it's so difficult for you to understand that we have to show you in practical terms. These two are able, as swiftly as they changed, to rescue people, provided that the distressed *shall* continue living."

I was bewildered, but filled as well with feelings of joy and excitement seeing this marvelous banquet. Angels not only exist, but they are a fact to be reckoned with in this entire Universe and in other Universes. They live in a world of complete beauty. The Angels have tasks within an amazing number of areas, and each of them performs their task with wholly Unconditional Love. Many good humans on Earth are taken directly to the Angelic Realm when they die. If they like, they can become Help-Angels or Guardian Angels. They may also choose other training.

"Many good humans become Angels," I commented on Zar's long story about Angels. "I don't think I'm any good, or not in my last incarnation, anyway. I was a rascal and I was good at scolding …"

"Be quiet, Jan!" Zar urged. "We are not talking about your outer expression. He is not sitting here now. Nobody is too insignificant or ignorant to help in our Worlds. But we insist upon compassion and love, even if it's so deep inside that we have to use pincers to pull it out."

Suddenly everyone at the tables stood up and sang something which sounded like "Hail" and "Kyrie eleison." It left me feeling very solemn.

From one of the balconies up near the roof of the pyramid, a staircase descended to the hall. A troop of figures dressed in blue came down the stairs. The troop came past the tables, directly towards us.

"Look at your clothes," Shala whispered.

I looked at my cloak. It was like a burnous, I thought, reaching my feet and with a belt around the middle. I've always wondered how Arabs can bear to wear these cloaks. What if they had to run? What are they wearing underneath? Anyway, here my cloak felt light and comfortable, so I wasn't complaining. Mine was shining blue. I discovered that my cloak was the only blue one within sight, except for the group approaching our table. That was a bit weird, of course.

The group stopped in front of me. The music stopped. It was totally silent in the big hall. I examined the group of figures – men and women, all dressed in the same kind of blue cloaks as mine. I was shocked. I knew them! Every face that smiled at me belonged to a close friend or relative of mine. I started to cry, and hugged them one after another.

"This is your Soul Group, Jan!" Zar explained.

My Soul Group! All my dearest friends! People who had lived with me both here and on Earth. The joy of this reunion was almost too much for me! But they all sat down at our table and the banquet continued.

Now I remembered. It was like a veil falling from my eyes and I understood where I belonged, who I was. These people – for me they were humans – and I were united by inseparable bonds. We were a big group, but not all of us were there; some were still on Earth. Now I remembered every single one of them, what they meant to me, why we had incarnated together, and all the wonderful plans we had had for the coming life. We had not succeeded in accomplishing our great plans on Earth. Our wills, the differences between us in both character and behavior, had made us strangers on Earth. Yet sometimes we were very close, bound together by a memory we didn't really have. It was there, in the depths, but the depths were unclear.

At this juncture, I also knew intuitively that my medium on Earth belonged to this group too, and that was why she was clever enough to perceive me. We all knew that it wasn't certain our message from here would reach Earth, and then we would have to make a new start.

We had climbed mountains together, physical and psychic ones. We also knew that we are able to influence and help those of us who are still living on Earth.

It was too wonderful to be true! I cried and I laughed, and we talked a lot without saying a word. It was quite a loud exchange of thoughts. When you are used to communicating telepathically you don't notice the difference.

My Soul Group was wearing different nuances of blue. Every face was so distinct, so well-known, so beloved. Not that all of us were relatives or closely related. I found only one relative that had been very close to me in my last incarnation, but who died a premature death – my dear sister Karin. It was such a joy to find her among the blue ones!

About Soul Groups and Twin Souls

What is a Soul Group? It is something so important, dear reader, that you must try to understand every word I say now:

A Soul Group is a group of between 25 and 50 individuals. All of them are Angels on this side, but not all of them have necessarily fulfilled their karma on Earth. Often a small group is taken out of the Soul Group and has the mission of incarnating on Earth at the same time. Some of them are older, some younger, but sooner or later they will meet and recognize each other. The sense of recognition among them is very strong. Nowadays on Earth many groups like this have met and understood that they must stay together and that they have a common task.

All this is difficult to explain without knowing how much consciousness has developed for some and how many are just marking time. There are many different factors to take into consideration, but most important is how people think. There are individuals belonging to a Soul Group who for various reasons block out their thoughts, thereby isolating themselves from the others. If so, it's important that somebody from the group recognizes them and helps them to wake up. In the Angelic Realm in the Ethereal World they will always be guided to their own Soul Group when they have crossed over. Some of them may need a little more training before that in order to have a successful reunion. I did.

You will need a highly raised consciousness if you go directly from

Earth to the Ethereal World. You can never be sure that all those people who boast about their contacts with Masters and Archangels really have this raised consciousness. It's possible that these "false" prophets belong to a Soul Group, which they long for without understanding what they are looking for. This is where the ego comes into the picture, and it could be easy for them to get on the wrong track. Some Soul Groups often work with their lost sheep, to get them on the right path before and after the crossing. But now positive things are happening because people are beginning to wake up. Soul Groups have succeeded in influencing their sisters and brothers on Earth into recognition. Very often the result of this has been the formation of groups. There will be a new epoch on Earth, when all these groups will keep alive the traditions, the connection and fellowship with their kindred souls here. This way many groups will come together, strengthening the bonds between Heaven and Earth. Some Angels in the Soul Groups may also be connected to other planets.

Does every human being belong to a Soul Group? the reader of course will be wondering. The answer is no. Did you ever ask yourself this question: "Who am I and what am I going to do with my life?" If you have, perhaps you have been sent to Earth with a mission from my friends here. The people belonging to a Soul Group come from the Angelic Realm without knowing that they belong there. It's always a question of intuition, because the subconscious mind holds all the cards.

What can be achieved by an Earthly Soul Group if some of them successfully find and recognize each other? Answer: meditation, assistance like healing, and conversation. There may be various actions together and even a network between the groups. It's difficult to give advice, because so few people know that they belong to a Soul Group. This kind of work is badly needed in the cities. Cities destroy people. Slowly a migration must take place towards the countryside and natural living. Nature plays an important role in the development of people, because if you live in harmony with Nature, you will have a keen ear for messages that come from a Soul Group.

The Soul Groups in the Angelic Realm have different colors or symbols. Like I said, there may be a great number of members. But just imagine that seven or eight people on Earth recognize each other and know they belong together. In that case, one of the members might claim that her best friend also belongs to the group, but the others will not accept this. So it's not possible to form Soul Groups on Earth. There must be an irrevocable, unquestionable recognition from deep inside the hearts of two members to be a solid sign of affinity. If there is a third party, this person must feel the same for the other two persons and vice versa. It's slightly complicated, isn't it?

Another important thing is the Earthly misunderstanding of Twin Souls. During my last years on Earth, in the 1960s, expressions like Twin Soul or Dual or Twin Flame were popular. Let me give you a new definition here.

The members of a Soul Group follow each other for centuries or millennia and they become totally linked to each other, whether they live here or on another planet. What is more natural than the recognition between two people of different sexes and the same Soul Group when they meet somewhere else than here and call themselves Twin Souls? Here all of us are Twin Souls, but I prefer to call it brothers and sisters. Duals are quite another thing. Every human being is a Dual, that is to say a male and a female entity, who very seldom go down to Earth together.

I mentioned above that here all of us are Twin Souls. This is not entirely correct. Every individual keeps his or her individuality here. We are composed in the same way you are and we often take our heritage with us when we pass over. We choose our parents on Earth. You have to be alert and able to withstand all the negative qualities there are in hereditary factors. How many people can do that – Soul Group members or not?

I cannot describe how I enjoyed the rest of my visit to the Angelic pyramid. It had such a light, melodious, and loving atmosphere. I again became one with my Soul Group. At last we had to say farewell, because I was still a pupil in the Angels' School. Zar comforted me.

"You will soon be reunited with your Soul Group," he promised, "but in order to be able to describe your existence here you will have to travel a little further with us."

12. Meeting with the Master Djwal Khul

There is a marvelous city in the Ethereal World. It has been talked and written about throughout the ages and is often called "The Golden City." We didn't need Jolith's soft wings to get there. The golden city Shamballa borders on the Angelic Realm, and as far as I can understand this gigantic city is quite a Realm in itself. It is the center of the Great White Brotherhood and all the other great Masters. Shamballa is the divine place for truth, wisdom, and Love.

I told you that it was easy to get there. I closed my eyes and Zar took one hand and Shala the other. I opened my eyes and we were there. We were surrounded by a golden haze. Through this haze I caught a glimpse of beautiful, tall buildings, surpassing ancient Roman and Greek architecture. A while ago I found the fantastic glass pyramid in the Angelic Realm a masterpiece of architecture – now I was standing in a city filled with similar masterpieces. The streets were paved with a yellow, shining material that resembled gold. The colors and the shapes of the buildings varied, but each construction formed a lovely pattern with the surroundings. Fountains played everywhere and multicolored flowers bloomed from well-laid flower beds. Graceful flowering trees made oases of shade and fragrance. There were tables and chairs, and we sat down in an arbor. When I listened I thought I heard the roaring sea in the distance. A silver-colored eagle fluttered high above our heads and it made me think of the huge mountains at home.

"You always compare things with Earth," Shala scolded me. "Here there are seas and mountains and forests – whatever you like. Shamballa is a jewel, located in the middle of the countryside. The city is also a retreat for highly developed Souls, like Sananda, Melchizedek, Buddha, Lord Maitreya, Lord Maha Chohan, and many others."

"Don't some of them go down to Earth and materialize?" I asked.

"It happens," Zar answered. "There are trustworthy men and women on Earth who have experienced blessed messages from the Masters."

"What are they doing here?" I asked a little irreverently. "Do they meet here and talk about how terrible human beings are?"

Shala put her hand to her mouth. She always did that when she was giggling. "You will never realize how much work is performed in this city," she said mildly. "The Masters are extraordinary administrators. Together with the Great Spirit and the Angelic Realm, they are our hope for saving the Earth."

"I can't understand why Mother Earth hasn't been saved yet, with such mighty powers on her side," I objected daringly.

"Come on, Jan!" commanded Zar, and he gave me his hand. "You and I must go on a trip together, and now would seem as good a time as any."

He took me to one of the nearest houses. When we came through the door it seemed to be a railway station. I couldn't see any rails, but there were several tunnel entrances.

"This is worse than the underground in Stockholm," I muttered when Zar took me into one of the tunnels. I was thinking as always, 'If I have to experience uncanny things, it's just as well to be already dead!'

The Journey to Earth

The tunnel was well-lit. There were vehicles parked on one side. Zar pulled out one of them and I was astonished. The wagon reminded me of those that you find on the roller-coaster in an amusement park, even if it was much more comfortable. There were two seats into which you sank deeply when you sat down. You sat in a small glass cage with a roof above you and windows all around you. Zar put on our safety belts and pressed a button in front of him. We shot away as if from a gun, right down a tunnel that seemed infinitely long. Zar glanced furtively at me and laughed.

"There's nothing dangerous here," he assured me. "We are driving in an underground tunnel."

There was not much to see, and this breakneck speed made me drowsy. I don't know if we stopped after one hour or twenty. When we did, we were still in the tunnel and I was somewhat dazed. Ethereal bodies can also get dizzy!

Later I realized that we had come out of a mountain opening. I was dazzled in the broad daylight. Zar put his hand over my eyes and then I felt better.

"Our underground tunnel system extends all over the Earth," he told me. "Now we are in Tibet."

An unusual yet stunningly beautiful landscape lay before us. We were standing on a ledge with stairs cut into the rock, which led down into a valley. A river ran down below through the long valley and turned sharply just where we came out. Slender trees climbed the green slopes. There was a moored boat right below us and there was a small house on a protruding part of the cliff. We saw a couple of larger buildings further away. We had come to a solitary place, yet it seemed to be full of life and joy.

"Have we taken the underground from the ethereal plane to Earth and further on under the crust?" I asked, again confused. "And we ended up in Tibet?"

"Oh yes," Zar answered happily. "You were sound asleep and you never noticed the transition. We passed through fog, just like when you're flying, and then we landed on Earth. Jan, this is a physical landscape. We are going to visit an old Master. He has lots to teach you!"

An small, elderly man came out from the little house on the cliff. First he embraced Zar, then me. I had to bend down in order to hug him.

"Welcome to my little oasis!" the old man said, and smiled with his whole face. He was not handsome, but I never saw such beautiful eyes as his, and his whole person radiated love and joy.

"My name is Djwal Khul," the Master continued, and invited us into the house. It was bigger than it seemed from the outside. There was a big library that I would have liked to investigate, but Djwal Khul asked us to sit down in a small room nearby, where there was a nice sofa and a huge window looking out over the river and the mountains. It felt like sitting in the middle of the rushing water of the river.

"Well," the small Master said, looking at me with his large, slanting eyes, "you've been wondering what the Masters are doing. And of course, now you are wondering what an ugly old man like me is doing here, in the wilderness."

I nodded. Sometimes I put my foot in it whatever I say. I didn't want that to happen now.

"There are several Masters from the Brotherhood who live in this valley in physical houses," Djwal Khul continued, "but we are not always physical." He put three small cups of strong sweet tea and a dish of delicious brown cakes in front of us. I immediately helped myself to one of the cakes, even if I had to pretend to eat it.

"We travel around in the tunnels and go wherever we are needed," the Tibetan Master explained. "Sometimes we are in Shamballa or on Sirius. You see, young man, that we work very hard. We all do that in the Ethereal World, both Angels and Masters. Many of us are teachers. Others are caretakers of energy, creators of energy, or cleaners of energy. We all have our missions to perform, be it on Earth or on another planet. We influence people or groups in a positive way. We inspire authors, something you should know about, and we try to save dying cultures. We don't only work by meditation, but also with practical physical and psychic work. Many of us have secret sanctuaries on Earth, like this one. We seldom rest. Good energies, frequencies of various kinds, and radiation are needed everywhere."

"I don't understand it at all!" I cried. "If you influence people in all these ways, things must happen."

"Well, don't they?" was the mild question.

"Well," I replied, "I believe you cannot influence the natural development of a human's brain. That is forced on by a human's free will, I suppose?"

"You probably know everything about human chakras," the small

Tibetan answered patiently. "Very few humans know how to charge their chakras. Chakras are power-centers, but in spite of that they seldom function the right way. There are certain exercises that must be done regularly. People stubbornly refuse to work on their thinking. Yet thinking is what guides them and what awakens sleeping chakras and potencies that lie fallow. The consciousness that people can activate their thoughts is yet too diffuse. A few people on Earth already know this and try to teach others, but the reception is too weak and without nuances.

"Many of us know that thoughts are creative. Thoughts create with a tremendous power if they are collected from the right source. I mentioned the word radiation earlier, and I meant radiation of thoughts. It is considered an important science by us, the brothers in the Great White Brotherhood. Every thought contains certain potencies. Every potency contains a quantum power. If you divide the potencies into two different thoughts, there is a huge reduction in power. For instance, a simple thought like 'Where did I put my pen?' can be compared with 'I totally trust in the divine and will immediately get my pen back!' In the first thought there is fear and irritation. Such thoughts erase power. In the second thought there is complete trust and assurance of getting the pen back without demanding anything or feeling worried."

"This is truly instructive," I sighed. "But the thing is, people don't remember to think in a cosmic way when they lose their pens. They are just cross at losing them. Who will help them think right, then?"

"I will, the other Masters will, and the Angels will. It's written in many books, Jan," Djwal Khul swiftly answered. "In one way you're right: It's the reception of the message and the memory that must be influential. We use radiation for that. Free will also plays its part. That's why we can't influence the whole of humanity. It must be done in small portions so that humans react with their thoughts. They must realize themselves what thinking means and how to use it in daily life."

"I inspire my medium on Earth with my thoughts," I remarked. "That's how I write now, through a medium. Can she influence me too?"

"Let us hope she can't!" exclaimed Djwal Khul, and all three of us started to laugh.

"Right thoughts have an enormous penetrating power," Zar remarked. "Jan, have you never experienced a moment of euphoric happiness?"

"Of course I have!" I replied and smiled, thinking of those happy moments.

"I don't mean sex," Djwal Khul objected treacherously. He must have thought-read my flight of fancy. "A special place, some music, and a kind word from a friend can also cause euphoric feelings. But okay, take sex as an example! At the moment of orgasm, the human is lifted and thought is dizzying. The thought is vibrating and everything floats into light. That shows some of the power I refer to. Miracles are only proof of the power of thought over matter. Everyone who completely has understood this has been able to perform miracles."

"I think it's a miracle that you can change in and out in your physical body," I said admiringly. "This landscape is physical and really exists, and you are here looking Earthly, so you must be able to change your physical body any way you like – or your ethereal one? I just don't get it."

"How do I look?" Zar asked. "Physical or ethereal?"

I looked at my dear guide and friend. He must have changed his clothes while I was talking to the Tibetan. Zar was dressed in an elegant white suit, with elegant white, pointed shoes with silver buckles. On the chair at his side was a tropical helmet. His white shirt was open at the neck, revealing a gorgeous jewel: a big blue sapphire surrounded by diamonds.

"You look like a lord, Zar!" I exclaimed. "When … how … did you change?"

I looked down at my own body, but I was still wearing my blue "nightshirt." Why did I not have Earthly clothes like my guide?

"I *am* a lord," Zar answered, with a broad smile. "My real name is lord Zarayan, but I seldom use it. I changed when you were deep in conversation with our host. I didn't only change my clothes; I also changed into my physical, Earthly body."

"No way. Now I am jealous!" I cried. "Here I am invisible and unable to eat nice cakes, and you are both physical. This is way beyond me."

"You will soon be able to understand it." Zar smiled. "Djwal Khul and I can see you even in your ethereal body, but we are trained to do that."

How to Materialize and Dematerialize

"I had a very definite purpose bringing you to this remote place on Earth, where my old friend and teacher lives," Zar continued. "Jan, it's time for you to learn materialization and dematerialization. You call yourself 'dead,' although you are very much alive. There are a few people on Earth who can dematerialize their bodies and visit our Worlds, but there are not many. It's much more difficult for a physical person to learn this, but for you I imagine it will be child's play! But it demands much self-discipline and practice. It's not difficult to materialize for a short time, as I did now. The Master Djwal Khul once taught me how, and now it's your turn to learn."

"Now?" I stammered, "Can I learn this *now*?"

"Of course, my boy," the old Tibetan said, and put his thin hands on my transparent shoulders. "Now you must listen carefully to what I say and do exactly what I teach you. Relax, and sit down comfortably on my sofa. When you dematerialize a physical body, you work with your cells so that they transform into a special light-energy. We'll now teach you to do exactly the opposite!"

It is impossible to describe exactly what happened next, but I will try as far as I can. I listened hard to the soft, guttural voice of Djwal Khul, who told me to perform certain moments of thought. The first thing was that I must think of my body, ethereal as it was, as consisting of cells, in this case light-cells. He showed me the cell-structure mentally and asked me to keep it in my thoughts. This way I imprinted the cell-structure of my body on my retina. At first I just saw it in light. The cells were distinct, but they were made up of a lot of light particles. The light became rose-colored and then pale rose. I still saw the structure distinctly, in the shape of my own body. I repeat: My own well-known

123

body took on a dense, bright appearance, made of light-red cells.

The Master told me to slowly build an aura around this body in the usual aura-colors: red, orange, yellow, green, blue, and violet. I looked at myself as if I were a dummy made of cells and tightly surrounded by the aura. At the same time I *was* this dummy.

I lowered the frequency. I felt like I was standing in the center of a vortex, whirling first at top speed, then slowing down until it stopped. I suddenly felt very warm and I was asked to put my hand in Zar's and open my eyes, which had been closed all the time. This procedure seemed to last for an hour, but it really took only a few minutes. I stared at my hand, which felt strange in Zar's strong grip. I put the other hand on my heart and felt it beating. I was neither dead nor spirit any longer! The physical Jan was back on Earth again. I felt very hungry!

Both teachers helped me up, and there I was standing on trembling legs. I didn't dare ask how long this change would last, I just enjoyed it. Or what was I feeling? Perhaps I imagined that I enjoyed being a living person again. Could I really be more alive than in my ethereal body?

We went into another room, where a delicious vegetarian meal was waiting. I ate and drank with a good appetite, and my teachers looked at each other and tried to keep a straight face.

"After dinner you will have to return to your ethereal state," Djwal Khul said. "The physical Jan must learn to go back to his unphysical life, because that is your rightful place. How does it feel to be dressed normally?"

I had completely forgotten to look at myself. I had on light-colored trousers and a white shirt. On top of this I was wearing a beautiful, embroidered waist-coat.

"This is the height of fashion right now." Zar smiled when he saw my surprise. "We cheated a little when we helped you to dress. You cannot learn everything at once, but it was fun that you didn't notice. That means that you were really concentrating on building cells. Now you must learn to dissolve them."

At first I was uncomfortable knowing that both Masters were laughing at me, and then we had a good laugh together. Time passed much too quickly in their interesting company, and soon my physical body had to relax again on the sofa. I tried chewing the last grape for a long time, but it didn't help.

"Now again you must think of your body as consisting of light-red cells, surrounded by the aura," Djwal Khul said. "It is very important that you see the aura distinctly. Visualize the aura-colors but also the magnetic field nearest your body. It looks like a field of pale yellow energy. The magnetic field belongs to your physical body. The whole time you must visualize your chakras and fill them with their respective light-colors. See how your cell-structure pales and turns into pure light. Pull this light the way I show you here: at first through the magnetic field and then up through the whole aura. Then steer it towards your interior until the aura has 'devoured' the cells. Now only your light body is there. Do you see?"

It was not easy to understand, but everything happened very slowly and I concentrated a long time on each of the different steps. I felt as if I was sucked upward or inward, but I didn't feel as if I'd vanished. The whole time I was conscious of what was happening and I was aware of my limbs and my whole body. My body was still there, but it became lighter and more flexible. When you die you don't know how the transition from physical body to non-physical body happens. It was difficult to understand how my body could be buried in the ground and at the same time become physical in a secret place in Tibet. Now I was Jan again: an Angel in a long, blue shirt.

"The body of your latest incarnation has moldered away in the earth," the Tibetan said, when he read the questions in my poor head. "You had to give yourself a new physical body. It was natural for you to materialize a body that resembled the one you had the last time on Earth. This one was younger and healthier, because these substitute bodies we create must be in good working condition. Not everyone can be an Ascended Master, even if Ascension is becoming quite a popular word on Earth. The time will come when some people are allowed leave Earth and bring their bodies with them. But that's another story."

"In due course you will easily be able to move in matter and walk in and out of your ethereal body when it is needed," Zar stated. "But never count on a long visit in the physical world; your substitute body cannot manage that. You will have missions to perform, and after that you come back."

"I once saw a film called Lost Horizon," I answered. "In the end an ethereal woman followed her beloved back to the physical world, but at once she lost her 'physical' body and aged a hundred years in a couple of minutes. Now I understand why. Perhaps the author of the book and the film was wiser that I gave them credit for. Now I choose not to return to Earth for any longer period. I really enjoy my life on 'the other side.'"

"Good!" Zar exclaimed with emphasis. "Say good-bye to our host and we will return home."

13. Back to Shamballa

When we got back to Shamballa through the tunnels, I believed that everything I'd experienced with the Tibetan was a dream. I told Zar my thoughts but he just laughed and told me that everything that had happened was as realistic as you could wish for when you were a traveler in two worlds. It was already a long time since I passed the Realms of Dreams, and the reality of the Ethereal World now seemed much more alive than the physical life on Earth.

When we met Shala in Shamballa I hugged her very warmly because I wanted to feel where I really was. She loosened my hard grip with a laugh and said, "What happened to you? You went away for a short moment!"

I suppose I still had so much in me from the Earthly Jan that I hadn't adapted to the rhythm of time here. Or was my confusion temporary?

"Your reaction is completely natural," Zar comforted me. "You have had a rather subversive experience and your body has not yet learned to follow the dissolving and the re-stabilizing of the cell-structure and vice versa. There are several levels of materialization. You learned the first one. It affected your mind temporarily but you will soon be better. Still, you cannot entirely control one of the great Cosmic Laws, but it is a good start."

"Our DNA is in the genes, which are in the cells," I wondered. "DNA is my identity-mark in my physical body. What identity-mark do I have, either in a substitute body I create but which doesn't exist, or in this ethereal body?"

"Hm," Zar pondered. "Good question. Bodies that are substitutes need no DNA, because they are not permanent and not given birth to by a woman. Look at the substitute body as a kind of robot where your soul is just visiting in order to bring life to a physical structure. In this body your identity mark is your *monad,* your immortal spark of life, the one you saw floating in the Cosmos at the beginning of all time. That is the most important identity-mark that exists, Jan. Remember that!"

We were walking along, talking on the golden streets. I was deep in my thoughts and wasn't looking around me, when suddenly we were standing in front of an enormous cathedral. Again I wondered if I had ever seen such a beautiful building. Not even my favorite cathedral in Chartres had such noble lines, such exquisite mosque-like roofs as this one. There are also beautiful churches in Russia, but this one beat all churches I had ever seen.

"Such a wonderful church!" I exclaimed, and took a step backwards.

"Church?" Shala asked, and laughed in her happy way. "We have no churches here. This is the Council Hall."

"Council Hall?" I asked. "What a strange town hall!"

"Not exactly," Zar corrected. "This is the Council Hall. It's the most important building in Shamballa. We have no priests and no churches. Why should we need them? We were all created by the Great Spirit. All of us are his children. We meet in the Council Hall when we have a council. Sometimes the Great Spirit visits us; on other occasions the Elohim and the Archangels come here. Sometimes the Nine Elders are visiting us from Sirius. Come on, we'll go inside."

I cannot describe what I saw, it's impossible. This house was not like a castle, with a gaudy interior and decoration that is beautiful only to the human eye. Why would I try to describe the most sublime of buildings, when words fail me? The reader must be content with trying to understand that colors, music, and scents can be united into something more than you can ever imagine: an atmosphere so sacred, yet so warm and full of love, that unaccustomed eyes were filled with tears.

I have read about Shamballa, I had theories about it when I lived on Earth, but I never ever came anywhere close to this.

Shamballa is not only a golden city with pretty gardens and lovely houses. If I am allowed to classify them, Shamballa is inhabited by the highest of spirits. I knew that I wasn't staying in this paradise, but before I left it, I experienced meetings that stayed in my mind forever, even if my mind is ethereal nowadays.

You arrive in a place like this with the leftovers of your unpolished manners as a human, such as the ones I brought from the coarse artistic circles of Stockholm. I have sat in smoky artist dens discussing life, without knowing the meaning of *eternal* life. I have drudged as a shopkeeper. I have mucked out the pigs while noble men sat drinking their evening brandy and soda on their verandas, looking out over their vast estates without giving a thought to who is cutting their grass or tending their gardens – let alone thinking of who was looking after their cattle in the pastures. I wonder where my beautiful country is going now, as I fall on my knees in silent admiration at the altar of Beauty. Is there someone out there who understands?

"It must have cost a fortune to build this magnificent palace!" I thoughtlessly murmured as we wandered around the halls.

"You should have learned about the power of thought by now," Zar admonished. "The whole of Shamballa is created by powers that have absolutely nothing to do with economics – or slavery. The city is built for and by the Masters in conjunction with the Great Spirit. It was made so long ago that you are unable to understand it."

I felt a little ashamed and I wondered why I was always comparing everything with Earth. Perhaps it is because I am writing this book, and that way, I have a connection to my old life.

We had sat down on a sofa for a little while and so my thoughts necessarily went back to dirt and envy. Suddenly a tall, blonde woman was standing in front of us. I recognized her immediately, even if it was a long time since we met.

It was Helia, the Spider-Woman, the Mother of Earth.

"Welcome back to the Worlds of Light, Jan!" she greeted me. "You have struggled on Earth life after life, but now it's all over. At your own request, you are granted the immortality you once sang about and longed for. Now you are allowed to create a future here with the help of your thoughts and readiness to learn. You are an adept of the

Masters and you belong to a Soul Group you know well and are used to working with. You will continue to do that, but you will have no further life on Earth. You wear the deep blue cloak, which means you will stay here. Only a few of your friends wear it too. Your teachers have shown you Shamballa, because even if you will live in the Angelic Realm, you need to know the way here. Perhaps you will need to use your substitute body in order to materialize on Earth, but as long as you are an adept you may only do it under our jurisdiction. Zar and Shala will guide you and help you as long as you need them. You know where to find me if you need me."

My Home Is in the Angelic Realm

She hugged me and disappeared as suddenly as she had come. Soon after that, we left the magnificent palace.

I felt more at home in the Angelic Realm than with the Masters. I always had some difficulties bending my long spine, and even if that wasn't needed in Shamballa, I couldn't completely be myself there. The solemnity was rather suffocating. There is humor, warmth, laughter, and tears in the Angelic Realm – all things humans are used to. Everybody helps each other and everybody has interesting things to tell. You learn a lot of new things. My visit to Tibet of course was thrilling, and I wouldn't say no to another visit. The Tibetan Master promised to see me again, and I look forward to that. I have many more things to learn from him.

I am dictating this book to my medium from the Angelic Realm. According to human chronology, I have been here about forty years, but days and nights here do not depend on Sun and Moon and we don't divide day and night as you do. We live in the wholeness. Your Gregorian calendar does not suit The People of the Sun and the Stars. They count time almost in the same way as the Mayans. You ought to do that, too. But the way Earth looks today there will be no changing time, even if it is variable.

130

I can understand that you want to know more about my life here. I am going to tell you about it now. If you don't believe me you must wait until you come here yourself. But it isn't likely that you will experience the same things as I have done. You may get quite a different idea of it all. And in that case I hope it's a positive experience!

The Angelic Realm is so big, it can't be measured in Earthly measurements. Here everything is in perfect order, which is reflected in our way of living, nature, and working methods. Everyone gets different tasks here, and I had to start from the beginning to learn the different ways of being an Angel. The first thing I learned was to move myself with the power of thought and to create wings. We *have* an ethereal body if we like, or else we can appear just as light. I prefer to have a body, even if it is very light and unphysical. Since my mental capability still remains, it feels strange to run around without a body. Well, that's my personal opinion, of course. I also like to be able to look at the person I'm talking to. If somebody starts a conversation without my seeing him or her, I can be rather rude. I tell the person to show themselves or else … well, I'm not going to be common. Sometimes my Earthly side gets hold of me – but here they understand and forgive straight away.

I learned to meditate properly. It's easier here; my brain seems so clear. On Earth I often mixed daydreaming and meditation, which was not good for the job I was doing at that point. Here meditation is classified as work. Just imagine: To sit comfortably alone or in a group and concentrate on helping somebody or perhaps the Earth, is work! I love when the concentration can create wings that you can fly with. What a happiness! I remember myself as a child, when I cut out wings from newspaper. I tried them on behind the barn, where no one could see me. I didn't know where the door led to, I just wanted to fly. So I jumped out into the wonderful air where my wings would support me – and instead I fell headlong into the dung heap. I would rather forget what followed!

Now my wings support me, even if they just are a kind of substitute engine for my light body. In fact, I don't need them, but because I have been given creative power (conditionally) I like to practice by taking a trip now and then. I don't actually need to do much more than think of a place – and like a shot I'm there. It's almost too comfortable!

It was difficult separating from my Guardian Angel Jolith. She was very happy. She had been close to me for such a long time, and now she was set free to work in another part of the Angelic Realm. You can choose if you want to remain a Guardian Angel or if you want to develop in other areas. What kind of areas, the reader will ask?

I soon understood that the Angelic Realm contained the most varied areas of work. In a high degree you could choose the area in which you had the most interest, but then you first had to get education or training that matched your personal wishes. For instance, if you want to stay on Earth as a helper you must first learn how to work invisibly. Invisible Angels wander around everywhere on Earth. But why don't they do anything, you might ask? Why don't they save people from diseases, accidents, drugs, violence? Why is there so much evil?

The answer is: because of human free will. Not even Angels can oppose it. And another thing: human karma. The Law of cause and effect is inexorable. Angels have lots of restrictions, because every human being has their own path to experience. But have you ever heard someone say, "He had a Guardian Angel?" You can be sure he did!

I am reunited with my Soul Group. There are only three of us who wear the deep blue cloak – two men and one woman. We work as teachers in the group. We went through the same school and learned everything from the beginning. We swam in the air-ocean as small sparks of life, and after that we joined the great, wonderful Creation. We didn't meet in my last life on Earth in Sweden, but we knew each other well from other incarnations. The man is called Henry and the woman's name is Tiri. All three of us are at different stages of development, and therefore we teach in very different ways.

I feel silly when I call myself an "Angel." Everybody who ends up in the Angelic Realm is called Angel, even if it doesn't correspond to the Earthly word. Angels are not an "ethereal people" or something that is described in the Bible. Angels are Lightworkers with very varied tasks.

Shala belongs to the Angelic Realm. Zar comes from the Masters

Realm. I had one of each kind so I could be guided and get developed for my task as a Lightworker. What that task is, I still haven't fully understood. I think the expression "you grow with your task" suits me well. I also think you can have several tasks, that gradually radiate out from the same core. They are part of the growing that continues for as long as you wish. But so far I love my job.

I tell my readers about the different Worlds and their Realms. Many authors have already done this. There are authors who, through a channel, describe their lives after death. It doesn't bear any resemblance to what I tell you. That is why the reader must use his own discernment and pick up those things which feel right. Each author has visited his own kind of World on this side. Each receiving medium thinks in his own way, interprets, and has his own ambitions. The important thing for all of us who supply messages from the World of Light is to make our light and our love alive for our readers.

I also think it important that every Soul Group teaches its wisdom in different words, because people are so different, assimilate things differently, wish and think different things. These differences are confusing. It is because of them that there are so many religions, when actually one God is enough, one Love knowledge. That's how it was meant from the beginning. Everything was simpler then. Today there is enormous confusion. You can see it in art, in music – in fact, in the whole community.

Earth is the main concern for the Angels. There are other planets that also need help, but none in such difficulties as Mother Earth. That's why I would like this book to be an answer to many cries for help, an answer that can comfort and soothe worried thoughts. I'm sorry to say that only those who listen can learn to think in a way that will set power on the right path.

14. Disobedience Is Punished

There is a word "precipitate." It is used to describe how you can realize your wish. I've always wanted to know how it worked. Now I know, but I didn't get that knowledge without pain. The word pain doesn't fit in the Angelic Realm, but even here you can do silly things. I could, anyway!

What I am going to tell you may sound like a fairy tale. Anyhow, I promise that this has happened to me "for real." It is one of the lessons that made me laugh a lot afterwards – but when it happened I wasn't laughing.

I now live in a wonderful little house. I didn't want a big, elegant house. I wanted to recreate something like my old farm cottage on Earth, which, in time, became our holiday cottage. I was able to write there – my imagination took off there, and I enjoyed every minute in this environment. It had grown into me. That was what I wanted for myself here too, because the Angelic Realm is a place of possibilities, where you create what you wish for. But the home was what caused all my problems.

When Shala and Zar left me with my Soul Group after the journey to Shamballa, Henry asked where I lived. If I had no home I could sleep at his house. He is a happy, easy-going person who radiates exuberant benevolence. I thanked him, because I had forgotten to ask Shala where I should live. Perhaps what followed was a test, even if I didn't realize it.

I went with Henry to his house. It was built in a castle style, and when he saw my surprise, he reminded me that we had incarnated together in just such a house and that his name had been Enrico. The palace was a creamy white and the front was like crushed nougat. Inside it was a massive nightmare. Henry probably loved exaggerated rococo, and there were gold and bows everywhere. I didn't want to hurt my old friend's feelings, so I gave him a kindly smile when he showed me where to sleep: a room of dazzling luxury, a four-poster bed with golden ornaments and "inspiring" paintings of bedroom scenes.

"How did you do this?" I asked carefully.

"It's all precipitated," he proudly answered. "Have you not learned that yet?"

"No," I answered, "only to materialize and dematerialize my body."

"What!" Henry cried and looked at me in surprise. "I haven't learned that yet. You must be a highly developed soul!"

"Let's not make comparisons," I warned. "We are all different, and that is why the Angels use different teaching methods. Do you really mean that this kind of palace can be built by your thoughts alone?"

"Not only palaces," Henry answered contentedly. "Everything, just everything! I can teach you. It is very simple."

"Do you think we are allowed to?" I asked, to be on the safe side. It was thrilling, and I had no intention of living in this marzipan cake for a long time.

"Of course," was his calm answer. "We belong to the same Soul Group, and it is natural to help and teach each other. It would be strange not to."

Henry was right. Precipitating was much simpler than materializing and dematerializing. It only took me a short while to understand how to do it, because I had learned to concentrate carefully. It was one of the first things you learned in the Angels' School. In order to precipitate you had to concentrate very deeply. You concentrate very hard on the thing you wish to manifest. Every detail of it must be ready in your thoughts when you start. We began with a few small things. I wanted a pair of white socks. You must need what you're wishing for if you want to succeed with the experiment. I looked at my bare feet in sandals, waved my toes a little, and felt how cold they were. In a moment a pair of thin white socks was lying in my hand. It worked!

The next thing I wished for was a bicycle. Henry roared with laughter.

136

"You don't need one here," he cried, as I happily cycled off. "You don't use bicycles here!"

I leaned my bicycle against a tree and went on with my own little sorcery. After a while, a big table stood in Henry's garden. On it were a bunch of carrots, a torch, a loaf of bread and a tub of butter, a pair of underpants, and a chamber pot.

"What a strange mixture," Henry muttered. "What are you going to do with all those things?"

"You told me to create small things before I started on the house," I reminded him. "I'm going to do the furniture. This is great fun! I could go on forever." I did. After a short while I was half-buried in household utensils, clothes, carpets, curtains, furniture, and tools.

Behind Henry's cream-puff of a house was a garden with a huge lawn, where we were doing all this. To my great surprise, Shala suddenly appeared. Henry and I were fully occupied with creating fancy goods. He was really skilled. Not even the creator of Meissen china could have told the difference between his own work and Henry's.

"What are you doing?" Shala cried. "Are you crazy? Are you precipitating for fun, big grown-up Angel-boys? Have you forgotten where you are? If Zar knew about this, I don't know what he would do. Having a laugh is one thing, but this is no joke, it is wasting the gifts of the Great Spirit. Watch me!"

In one single moment all we had created was destroyed, including Henry's cake castle and the garden.

"I came here to take care of you and see if our newcomer Jan had a bed to sleep in. What do I find? Two little boys playing with Creation. These are the kind of games which are destroying your Earth. Another term for it is abuse of power."

I fell on my knees in front of Shala. I felt so ashamed, I could not look her in the eye. She stood silently for a long time, looking at us. Henry was sitting on the ground with his hands covering his face. We were devastated.

"Get up!" Shala ordered. "I think your mere fright is punishment enough. Jan, you must promise me not to precipitate one more single thing before you have learned more about it in the Angels' School. This was a pathetic attempt at the real procedure, and what you created could just as easily disappear. Henry, you must create a more suitable dwelling. Your castle was too ostentatious. I can't believe you can still have such a silly attitude. We'll have to sort that out before you can go further. I will talk to your teachers."

She disappeared, and Henry and I looked at each other blankly. We hadn't intended any wrong; maybe that was why we were spared more punishment. Henry loved knick-knacks and I was as usual curious of my own capability. When we first came to the Angels' School, we learned self-control and simplicity. I was a master of the latter, but I had always lacked self-control, just like Henry.

When we returned to school we were punished with a walk through the different Realms of No Man's World in order to discover what the weaknesses in our characters could result in. I assure you that it was not a nice walk. We visited the dwellings of unblessed souls, hell or purgatory, whatever it's called, and we had to watch self-made suffering that leads nowhere. After that we went home to meditate on the contact with our Inner Self. I do not know how long this punishment went on – it seemed a very long time for both of us, even if it was only a few hours. During this time Tiri worked on much more exciting things. Sometimes she came to let us know what fun was in store for us. Tiri is a very captivating person.

I have never been very obedient. The spirit of rebellion lives in my breast, and is difficult to keep in check, even here. Zar, of course, knows about this. It was a long time after our mischief before I met him again, and it was a lonely time. Not even Shala appeared. At first I felt offended, and thought that friends need not abandon each other. Then I took a long look at my inner self. I realized that I had to demonstrate purity when I was studying with my teachers.

I worked hard during this time. I met near ones and dear ones who had passed the border but not yet incarnated again. When they were to "go down," I met with them and informed them of the importance of keeping a pure consciousness and filling their thoughts with love when they were born again. Each of them had a gift to take with them to Earth, a positive quality to manage and develop in the best way they could. Some of them were scared of being reborn but understood that it was necessary, because their karma was not fulfilled. I calmed them and gave them tasks that they hopefully would remember sometime on Earth. I distributed power and positive energies, I supported and encouraged them. These experiences took place in many different Worlds where I was called to take care of souls in various stages of development. At last, after an interesting and instructive time, I was ready again to meet Shala and Zar.

140

15. The Ashtar Command

"My dear friend!" Zar exclaimed, and embraced me. "When you lived on Earth you understood that you were responsible for your own life. When you had chosen your path you were responsible to yourself, to nobody else. Temporarily you were responsible for your family. You could never blame others when you had done something silly. To blame others is not accepted here. You have been called to account for exactly that. When you precipitated you secretly blamed Henry all the time. He was the one who taught you, he was guilty of your going too far because he took part in it. But here, in the Angelic Realm, you must be responsible for your own actions. If you can't take responsibility, you will have to move to a World where you can learn to understand that truth. You don't need to do that. We have looked into your heart and we know the inner Jan. You are on your way to learning who you are, something that every individual sometimes asks. Who am I? Why am I me? Will I always be me?"

"Oh yes," I eagerly interrupted, "those are questions I've asked myself many times."

"The answer is much easier than you think." Zar smiled. "You will find out in time; I won't serve it up for tea. Now we will continue your education on another level, and Shala and I will be with you the whole time. First we are going to travel together again. You will visit our military facilities on the outskirts of the Ethereal World."

"I was never more than a lance-corporal," I muttered.

"Soon you will meet several generals," Shala laughed.

"I must tell Jan something," Zar interrupted. "There is a galactic confederation that guards Earth in order to step in if nuclear attack threatens the planet and the surrounding ether. The space fleet on duty is known as the Ashtar Command. It is made up of members from the Masters and the Angelic Realms, as well as other planets, galaxies, and universes."

I don't know if I should describe what was now shown to me as a military base with an elongated citadel, or as a strange kind of airfield. It surrounded the whole of the Ethereal World and contained hangars, barracks for the various troops, large digital structures (so it seemed to my ignorant eyes), and much more. There were many kinds of buildings, extensive parklands, gardens, swimming pools, training fields, and enormous landing strips everywhere.

I saw individuals who did not appear particularly human. It was just like arriving in a science-fiction movie. Some of them resembled animals; some looked more traditionally humanoid, with tiny bodies and large heads, enormous eyes, and rudimentary noses, mouths, and ears. All these beings radiated Love. There was intense activity, yet in the middle of all this work, these beings came and embraced us in a very unmilitary way. To my great surprise I discovered that I could communicate with them. They seemed intelligent and quick-witted. I asked about their engines and other technical equipment. At that moment Zar interrupted.

"Shala and I are going," he said. "We'll leave you here for a while. It is a part of your education as an adept to take part in everything that goes on in the Ethereal World as well as in the other Worlds. If you work with the Ashtar Command for a while you will really learn work of unselfishness and Love. We will come for you when you are finished."

He was off like a shot and I was left standing there. But I had no time to ponder my situation. A young man in a white uniform patted me on the shoulder in a friendly way.

"I'm called Tone, and my job is to show you around here," he said. "Come with me, please!" He took me to my lodging, a cozy and comfortable room in one of the barracks I had seen during our flight.

"First I'll take you to the base," Tone continued. "The commander-in-chief wants to see you to give you your first mission."

The commander-in-chief looked like a Native American. He was dressed in the same white uniform as Tone, but his headdress was different. It was tall, with an ornate diadem of precious stones with long drops dangling at his sides and a bush of feathers, softly swinging in the breeze.

"Yes, I was an Indian chief in my last incarnation on Earth," he said, with a broad smile. (Of course, he had read my thoughts!) "Here I represent The People of the Sun and the Stars from Zio. As you can see, I come from a long way away, from the outskirts of the galaxy. I am well informed about everything which concerns this galaxy and what a bad state Earth is in. For the time being, you are going to be one of the light warriors in my army. Don't misinterpret the word 'warrior.' We are peaceful soldiers, and our most important weapon is Love. Is that clear, combatant?"

Oh dear, I thought, as my memories of being a soldier came back to me. But I straightened my insubstantial legs and saluted. The Indian chief, whose name was Kualli, as I got to know later on, looked at me in a friendly way.

"There is nothing to fear," he said. "Don't compare my regiment with those on Earth. Mechanical discipline is something for humans. Here everyone performs his duty and we have a good time together. It's very simple. You obey your inner voice, a voice that comes from the Great Spirit. That is the kind of obedience we expect from you."

I was very surprised when he embraced me and also Tone, who was standing at my side. Later on, when I asked Tone about my task, he answered with a broad smile, "You will simply belong to my unit. First you will be given suitable clothes, and after that you will meet the pals."

My new clothes were a white, tight-fitting, shimmering suit with a short cape. There was a round badge with symbols on it on my chest. It was very nicely made, and I fingered it with interest. Tone swiftly removed my fingers from the jewel.

"It's an alarm," he told me. "You couldn't know that. You press with various codes that you must learn. Here's a belt with pockets in it. There you keep a crystal for communication when you are far away. There is also a holster for a weapon that you will learn about later. Sometimes they are necessary. This is an amethyst-device that provides directions. It's a little like radar. It warns you when it is needed, and it can find every road in the whole galaxy."

I felt like I was back at school, but I soon became part of the gang and I was very surprised to find Tiri there. No male-domination here, then, I thought cheerfully as I embraced Tiri.

"No, there are several women here, as you can see," she laughed.

"None as beautiful as you," I whispered in her rosy ear. She took off the compulsory hood that we all wore and a cascade of red-gold curls fell down her neck. The hood was the same material as the suits. It was a tight fit and did not leave any hair loose. All of us had different emblems on our hoods. Coded too, for certain. To my delight, mine was an eagle. It is the bird I most admire. It symbolizes boldness and freedom, two qualities I've always recognized in myself.

What did we learn in this alternative "cadet school?" Answer: Everything! We prepared for a visit to Earth, we learned to materialize and dematerialize – although I already knew that. We learned to tackle all kinds of situations which might arise on our tasks as guardians. We learned to eliminate poisonous gas, to destroy other poisonous pollution anywhere in the atmosphere around the Earth which threatens the nearest planets and stars. The holes in the ozone layer must be mended or the rays of the Sun will kill instead of giving warmth. There must be watchmen, both on Earth and in the atmosphere around it, who can intervene in case of urgent catastrophes.

Mission North America

After all the philosophizing, it felt good to have more practical tasks. It was really nice when I was chosen for an important mission with Tiri. We were going to Earth in our ethereal bodies and we were not allowed to materialize unless absolutely necessary. The mission concerned a nuclear reactor in North America. It was a very serious task, because the reactor was running the risk of meltdown. We had to prevent such an accident. If it happened, it would cause more disaster than we could ever imagine. We were summoned to General Kualli to get instructions on how to go about it.

"Kualli means 'good' in Native American," Tiri whispered to me before entering the General's room.

"Good by name, good by nature," I whispered back.

"He is the best!" Tiri answered, and I felt very curious. Tone was there too. To my surprise the General himself was going to escort us.

"I will come with you and supervise," he told us. "Tone worked with nuclear power during his life on Earth. Jan knows Earth better than we do, and he has both sense and imagination. Tiri represents yin and she is also bold and ingenious. But first I will explain the strategy. A teacher will come and explain what to do, and then we will meet in hangar Tellus when you are ready for departure."

There was no time to lose. What happened now happened very swiftly, and our instructor for the journey to Earth was brief and efficient. We were given lots of information that we carried with us in a kind of microchip. We were soon sitting in a ship that reminded me of a UFO. I asked why we did not travel through the tunnels below Earth like I had with Zar. Kualli answered that the Ashtar Command uses only airborne craft and that the tunnels were used mostly by the Masters. I had butterflies in my stomach, going back to Mother Earth in this craft and also going "abroad." I had not been in the habit of visiting America. "Tall Jan" from old Sweden was now a beacon in more than one way. I've always considered Sweden the most beautiful country in the world – but then I had nothing to compare it with. Tiri came from New Zealand, but I couldn't think that far. She had the looks of a Swedish lass. Yes, she reminded me of one of the girls up at the mansion when I was a boy – the girls who were known as trainees. We, the boys, peeped at them on the sly.

It was night when we landed in a desert place. Our ethereal bodies could not be touched by the dangerous emission, in case that would happen. Without much difficulty we gained entry to the nuclear reactor. So there we were!

All four of us stood hand in hand in the gigantic building. This kind of power station had just started to show up during my last ten years of Earth life. Now I found myself in the middle of this dangerous building and was I curious! We didn't experience the atmosphere the same way as the physical humans did, but we really experienced the variety of human reactions. Some people worked silently and intently trying to prevent the meltdown, others were completely hysterical. Some just yelled. The catastrophe was about to happen when we intervened.

The leakage had started, even if it was on a small scale.

I will not weary my readers with the details of what we did, because my technical knowledge is not great. We don't want praise for saving the nuclear reactor, while some competent people risked their lives to save others. Tiri and I worked on the destruction of the dangerous poison before it could penetrate the people. We protected them with clean air-curtains and wrapped them up in clouds of ethereal tinctures of balsam, which penetrated their bodies and served as protection. Kualli and Tone entered the meltdown at once. I dare not imagine what they did there, but the leakage was stopped.

At one point it seemed that disaster was imminent. Tiri was so eager to help and save that she forgot about her invisibility. It can happen to any of us when we are excited – it has happened to me too. Tiri was helping a hysterical woman who was crying and crying. She tried to influence the woman mentally, but nothing helped. Tiri's loving attempts to penetrate the screaming with calming vibrations resulted in a sudden, unconscious materialization because of the strain. I was working in another part of the building, but I caught a glimpse of the outline of Tiri's physical form and hurried to her. I succeeded in averting the materialization and my unaware partner regained her ethereal form. Then I plunged the yelling woman into a deep sleep. Nobody had seen us, because there was so much going on. Someone took the sleeping woman and carried her out of the building. Tiri cried with relief.

Kualli praised me afterwards, but Tiri felt ashamed. She kept close to Tone on the journey home and I talked to Kualli. I increasingly admired and respected this remarkable man. He claimed that the humans on Earth must understand that they need to seek their origin, the old way of living together in peace and harmony – without this, there is no way of solving the problems of modern times. He told me about the situation of Native Americans in a way I had never heard before. The first people were becoming the last of their kind. The color of your skin defines your rights as a citizen. White-skinned people see themselves as superior to all the others; the white-skinned Adam is, according to the Bible, the first man on Earth, and woman is just a product of him. She is the temptation and the slave.

"But Adam was not the first man on Earth," Kualli maintained. "There were both men and women among The People of the Sun and the Stars. The skin color of the people from Zio was the result of pigment, not a reason for allotting value. All humans are worth the same. Love for the Creator and for each other is the only religion we should have."

This and much more the handsome Indian told us. He was only interested in one mission: to save the planet that originally belonged to The People of the Sun and the Stars. Every human being is descended from them. "You cannot re-create the ancient, but you can build something new and valuable that is accepted by the whole Earth," he said. I listened attentively.

"Well, General, where does Evil fit in?" I asked.

"Those who bring their evil, violence, abuse, and most of all their desire for power with them, those who live in evil and for evil will not remain on Earth. We have arranged a place for them on other planets, where they must learn to live in a new way and where they can atone for their crimes – especially violation of their own Self."

"What is the future for Earth?" I asked.

"Have you not heard about the 'changes?'" he answered, with a swift smile. "You must have heard of catastrophes, famines, wars and civil wars, floods, and earthquakes? Isn't that enough to explain that not only has Mother Earth had enough, but so has her Creator? Now we are guiding Earth towards a brighter future. We are called the Ashtar Command, but in reality we belong to the Command of the Great Spirit. Ashtar only takes orders from the Creator himself, and he is our link to the Great Spirit. The living heart of Earth is beating in our hands, and her tears are our power source. We are the knights of space and the spiritual warriors of Earth. It is with pride, joy, and humility that I thank you, my skilled co-workers, for your achievement today. There will be no dire consequences for earth and sea this time, but we must keep our eyes on nuclear power stations. In the background the risk of accidents due to human error always lurks."

Perhaps my readers think that I am lecturing? Be like this, do that, and you will be a worthy member of Our Lord's pasture. Try to understand that I do not mean to be sanctimonious, or to convince you of what is good or bad. I fully believe you know that yourself. I just want to tell you about all the wonderful and fantastic things I have experienced, and at the same time show you that I still have many human weaknesses. I will now tell you about one of them.

About Earthly Feelings and All-Love

When we returned to our beautiful barracks, a feast was waiting for us. Feasts take place frequently here, but they are not the drinking-bouts they are on Earth. We meet and eat and drink the cosmic way, and that means that our food is quite different from anything my readers can imagine. I can't really describe it. We listen to music and we experience light-theater. It's difficult to put our entertainment into words. Light-theater might be formatting of Angels to music, images in extraordinary colors and patterns, it could be song, speech, and of course dance.

I hurried to sit next to the lovely Tiri before somebody else did. She had avoided me consistently. "What's up with you?" I asked, rather indignantly. "I save your life and then you keep well away from me. Don't you know how much I like you?"

"That's exactly what I do know," she replied, and she started to laugh. "Saved my life – aren't you funny! When you helped me down there, your soul came so close to mine that I couldn't avoid feeling its radiation. Another dangerous radiation, Jan! I am grateful, and I like you, too. But among the first things we learned in Angels' School was to eliminate as much as we could from our personal ego-feelings, in order to be included in the Law of divine, Unconditional Love. Have you forgotten? We are not allowed to feel the personal, individual love between man and woman, Jan. Not the kind I felt coming from you. Desire belongs on Earth. We're allowed to love each other and live together here in perfect soul-love, but that's another thing."

"Yes, I know, and I understand that." I was irritated. "But I can't control my feelings when I see you. You even belong to my Soul Group, and it leaves me all in a dither."

"That is your problem." She smiled. "You also know that every soul has its Dual, and that's what it belongs to. There's no point being out on a spree while your flame is incarnating on Earth, as are both yours and mine. Just wait till we meet them! Maybe we can persuade them to stay with us in order to avoid heart-rending scenes like this."

Heart-rending scenes, I thought. I had obviously kept too many Jan-feelings of various sorts. When I looked up I saw Zar looking at me. He held his goblet high and I saw a roguish gleam in his eyes.

"It's all becoming clearer!" he shouted over the table. "You and I need to talk about feelings!" That's exactly what we did. A little later we sat together in a flowery arbor in the garden.

"The most important thing a human has is feelings," my dear leader said. "I am not a moralist, and there's no question of that sort, but feelings must be guided in the right direction. You know that! Falling in love, desire, and sex are all part of the suffering and the joy of life on Earth.

"We bring part of it with us, but here it's time to learn to sublimate those feelings. That doesn't mean that we'll get bored, does it? Here you will find all kinds of positive joy, dancing, playing, and singing – but not love-games. We have so much Love and *live* in it, so that it gives us energies stronger than the rays of the Sun. The energies we emanate are compressed Love. We emanate them to ourselves, to each other, to the Earth, to the whole Universe. These energies are tremendously active. With their help we are able to breathe and move. From them we derive all the talents we have. Do you understand?"

"I'm trying to, anyway," was my answer.

"Your feelings must be part of the Oneness," Zar went on. "From there they radiate out into the whole cosmos with the immense power of universal Love. That is how all of us work. But if your feelings overflow and become emotional tradesmen, offering their goods at sale price, you will destroy the power of the energies you emanate."

"That's a bit harsh, just because I like somebody a little more than someone else," I protested.

"You can like as many people as you want," Zar objected. "You and I and Shala like each other a lot. But you have not succeeded in processing your Earthly feelings yet. Most people keep these feelings even after the crossing, but many of them stay in the No Man's World or the Astral World. We need you here, in the Ethereal World. If you prefer living with your desires, you must go back to No Man's World, where there is a lot of that kind of thing. If you want to work with the Angels and with us, you must learn to control those feelings and instead work with your All-Love. It's your choice."

"Of course I choose to stay here," I muttered. I felt distressed at the harsh words, but later on I understood how important it is to learn to feel the right way. Feelings are important, but it is even more important to control them. Sublimating one's feelings is not done at the wave of an Angel's wing.

"You were allowed to retain the memory of your last life on Earth. This is necessary for some tasks, and especially for cooperation with your medium. Now you must return to Kualli, because you have not finished your 'military' education yet."

I was happy to stay with Kualli a little longer. I thought Tiri would be reassigned, but that was not the case. She belonged to Kualli's protégés as before. I cannot call us soldiers, because there was nothing soldier-like in the life we had in Ashtar Command's barracks. But there was a strict discipline, not because of strict orders, but because we all wanted it. Henry was in a completely different part of the gigantic space fleet. Since the regions of the Ashtar Command covered the whole Ethereal World, there were innumerable sections, military units, camps, and other activities.

If I had still been living on Earth and had fallen in love with a colleague, it would have ended in a relationship or being split up

150

with removal to separate departments. Here it was the opposite. You were confronted with the problem until it was eliminated. I put hard emotional demands on myself. I was the only one who could go inside myself and contact the Higher Self. That was what was expected of me. When Tiri was nearby, everything was twice as hard, but eventually I learned to meditate on this issue, and I created a different relationship between her and myself. She became a very good and true friend. I realized that this was the best solution. Neither of us would be deceived if our feelings took over. In the beginning they did. But I must admit that she was my best teacher for controlling feelings.

Controlling feelings may seem hard to human ears, but the words do not have the same meaning here as on Earth. Here everything is a merging into the Wholeness and an unselfish, unlimited feeling of Love, which is difficult to explain to a terrestrial. There, I've just invented a good word! Ashtar Command and visitors from other planets are extraterrestrials to you. To us you are, dear inhabitants of Planet Earth, terrestrials. That's a fitting word, because you have to be properly Earthed as long as you live on Tellus.

My tasks were many and far-reaching, and Tiri and I were often sent out together. Sometimes Tone went with us. Tone was a soul who I did not understand. There was a little discomfort between us Angels. He was so evasive; I couldn't get a hold on him. He often smiled instead of answering, and when we were on a mission together he would disappear without a word. He was definitely clever at what he did, but he seemed shy. He was quiet and friendly. Once he told us that he had died of cancer as the result of working in a nuclear power station in Russia. All my other friends were very kind, and most of them belonged to my Soul Group. We looked forward to the feasts we had after every successful mission. We danced and sang and enjoyed being together – and of course we still do.

I have told you about the nuclear power station. There were other missions, including stopping the development of floods, channeling water, and cleaning it. When major railway accidents and car accidents occurred and many people died, we had to check that the right people survived and give them courage and energy. Best of all, I liked the missions involving the dark, aromatic soil that I've loved since childhood. I loved to float around in the forests and prepare Nature Spirits for environmental problems and help them to clean the air, wind, and water, and many other things.

I was only sent on these kinds of missions for a short time. They were minor missions. Main missions involved preventing or at least reducing violence, hatred, and evil, mostly in the big cities. I didn't like big cities – perhaps that was why I was sent to Hong Kong, New York, London, Paris, Rome, and many others. Big cities are as unpleasant for a spirit as for a human, but I learned a lot. I was not allowed to materialize in these places. I was air in the air, even if the air of the cities was as thick as pancake mixture.

My First Pupil

Once, when Kualli called upon me, I had just come from Iraq. It was an unpleasant experience, even though I was there in a helping and preventive capacity, because moral disarmament was interspersed with an ominous warlike rearmament.

"You have done well for a long time now," Kualli greeted me, making me proud and happy. "Your missions have been related to Mother Earth, because you feel such a special affinity with her. I appreciate that, because I am as much an old Indian as you are a farm boy. My whole life on Earth was an initiation into Nature. But there will not be much Nature left if things do not change on Earth soon.

"I have a dream, Jan! I dream of new fresh grass growing on Earth and new fresh flowers poking their colorful heads up everywhere they can. I have a dream that water in lakes, rivers, and seas will be free of poison and that salmon and trout will dance in the brooks. I dream of people living together in small villages, peaceful in dialogue and deed. I dream of graceful willow trees, dipping their branches in the water while small children play with Nature's own toys on the beaches: stones, pine cones, and sticks. I can see an old man sitting among them. He is carving a beautiful boat and telling fairy tales and legends of old times. The children listen, because children always listen, if grownups haven't removed their capacity for listening.

"I dream of the mass-media used in a positive way, to help, teach, and delight people and also bring them knowledge of ancient cultures, forgotten habits, and rituals. I would like to give all this to Earth. The whole Ethereal World wants to see a new Earth, not just me. That's what we are working towards, what we hope for, and what we are trying to carry out.

"Jan, I have a new mission for you. I want you to take care of a young boy who has recently arrived here. He is from a Swedish incarnation and is called Lasse. He died in a motorbike accident that was arranged by his own gang, who call themselves Hell's Angels. Tone, bring the boy here!"

The General shouted the last sentence into the air, and suddenly Tone was there with a young man who looked very lost. He was tall and somewhat lanky, with fair, untidy hair down to his shoulders and his thin, pale face was far from friendly. He clenched his teeth and looked furtively at me. Yet there was quite a strong light around the boy. His face would be nicer if he smiled. His thin hands with long, beautiful fingers suggested an artist. I hugged him. He remained as stiff as a poker.

"Come with me," I suggested. "I will show you around." Inside, I wondered how a boy like this could end up in the Ethereal World and if he would really listen to me.

"How come you were murdered?" I asked him, while we were strolling in the park.

"They didn't like me," was his simple answer. "I mean my mates. I was interested in things they didn't understand: astrology, alchemy, all kinds of esoteric things."

I was surprised by this. I had not expected this kind of interest. But of course there must be a reason for him to be here.

"And now you want to stay here?" was my friendly question.

"Nope! I thought so at first, but now I miss Earth. Thought that I would get even with those bast ..." He stopped himself swearing and smiled uneasily. 'That's a beginning,' I thought.

"So, you want to carry on with drugs, violence, and evil?" I asked him coldly.

"I never said that!" He turned two big, dark blue and surprised eyes on me and the sullen face burst into a big, friendly smile. He looked beautiful all of a sudden.

"You want to get revenge for your murder," I exclaimed. "That's what you said."

"You can get revenge in several ways," he answered, still smiling. "I am going to get revenge with Love. I'm going to teach them what life is really about. They called me the Black Messiah, because their black souls had dark names for everything."

"You talk as if you had read a lot of books." I was astonished.

"I finished sixth form last year," he answered. "Got a bike from my dad, a Harley Davidson. So that was the choice: either join their Hell's Angels or be attacked by them every time I rode my bike. So I joined them. When I saw what they were doing I tried to reason with them. I was really in love with a girl who was with them, too. Because of her I tried to play the game, but in the end I couldn't hack it. Then it was goodbye. Five of them drove me into the wilderness. What hurt me most was that my girl was with them. It's kind of meaningless to be born to a missionary and not get the time to be one."

"And so you came up here?" I continued to ask.

"Up, well ... at first I thought I was going down. But there were lots of Angels around me. I always believed in Angels without the Hell's bit. Then, at last I realized I was on the right path. What are we going to do now?"

Now I laughed. What a wonderful lad! I really liked him.

"Are you not going to stay here?" I asked. "It's quite tough on Earth now. Who knows what will happen to you if you go there again."

"It's not that bad," he answered happily. "Now I know where I will come when I die. I like it here, but I need to go back. I'm not giving up that easily."

"Then you must be taught by me for a while," I warned him jestingly. "If you insist on going back to Earth you must bring something back.

154

You must have a task, a mission!"

"That sounds okay!" He whistled. "When do we begin?"

"Here and now!" I sounded very resolute. "You are now on a naval base under the Command of Ashtar. Ashtar is …"

"I know who Ashtar is," Lasse interrupted. "He is the chief of the whole space-gang. I have read a lot about those guys. But nothing about you or written by you."

"I had not expected that," I said. "You were born long after the time of my childhood. But now you have to learn things that you will bring to Earth. They will be filed in your subconscious mind. Do you wish to go back to Sweden?"

"Absolutely!" he answered with conviction. "Preferably to the same mum. And dad too. There was nothing wrong with dad except that he never had time for me, because he was a politician with parachute-contracts. He slaved his life away. Mum loved to read science fiction and New Age books. I want to be born in Sweden and later on I want go to the USA and study Native Americans. I like them!"

"That's okay, Lasse," I answered. "Native Americans are your origin. But you have to learn a lot before we let you leave. For instance, you must learn to be responsible for your own life. You are a unique individual, as is every human being. You have your aura, your karma, and your dreams. Never forget who you are, that you are here right now, and that you have your own free will. During childhood you need guidance and love. When you're grown up you get your own integrity and must be responsible for your actions. We cannot decide now which parents you will have this time. This is my basis for teaching you and if you like what you see, we will start now."

He liked it. And I had my first pupil in this huge, endless school!

I look back on my time with Lasse as something enriching and instructive for both of us. Sometimes Tiri was present and she brought something extra to our conversations. Lasse adored the earth on which she was floating and I laughed up my sleeve at the boy's yearning. I even shared in it. I was gradually beginning to understand myself, and for that I gave Lasse the credit. I also understood why Kualli had given me this boy as a pupil. I told the dear, old Indian chief so a little later and told him that I was happy that Henry's and my prank had brought me here.

"Do you really think that?" Kualli laughingly exclaimed. "Do you think that this is a convict-settlement? My dear friend, it is an honor and a distinction to take part in the Ashtar Command. Jan, we never punish, we restructure. We have always known that you have grit in you and that you are one of our most gifted adepts. We are happy that you like working here until it is time for a new posting."

"But I want to stay here," I stammered. "You are like a father to me, and a best friend. You are my ideal, a role-model I will always carry in my heart."

"All right, my boy," Kualli patted my shoulder. "Let's not exaggerate! We are all parts of the Wholeness. I will still be your friend after your move. You can see me whenever you want to, and I will be your adviser if you need one."

That was a consolation. I returned to my task with Lasse. He was very intelligent and he stored all knowledge in the right way, so that he could take it with him to Earth. On a similar theme, I want to tell the reader that the children who are born now and in the future bring wisdom from our Worlds, stored near the surface. It just needs a little nourishment to be revealed.

Lasse at last decided to be born to his own little sister, who had been fourteen years old when he died. Now she had married and was dreaming of a child. We had many long discussions how he was going to use the "luggage" he was bringing. The old culture of the Native Americans belonged to his plans for the future.

At last the moment came when I guided him to the place in the Angelic Realm where the "birth-chamber" was. There are birth-chambers in No Man's World, in the Astral Realm, and the Ethereal World, because in all these Worlds there are souls who either want to or have to return to Earth. A last hug, and after that loving Angels took Lasse to the beautiful chamber that was the terminus or the start – whatever you want to call it. My heart was heavy when I returned to the Angelic Realm. But a nice surprise was waiting for me there.

16. Helia and Sananda

The old cottage that I had loved so much when I lived on Earth was standing there, gray and worn in its simple beauty, among budding birches, mighty oaks with swollen buds, and the scent of cut grass. The ground under the trees was covered with wild blue anemones, white windflowers, and a few cowslips. Shala and Zar came out of my cottage and welcomed me. This was the reward for my lengthy and assiduous work for Kualli. My whole Soul Group also arrived, and we had an inaugural ceremony, the happiest one I'd ever experienced. The adept Jan would be beginning at a "higher" education, and I was grateful that I could sometimes creep into my cottage and just enjoy being in a beingness which goes far beyond the ability of human thought.

The Goddess Helia: The Virgin Mary

Zar was not my only teacher now. I was really happy to visit the Master Djwal Khul several times and I also met his colleagues. I accompanied Zar to the Nine Elders and I met the Master Sananda, alias Jesus the Christ. Perhaps this sounds bombastic and affected to the reader, but that was not the case. All these meetings were happy and cozy. I cannot tell you about all I saw and heard; it would be too extensive. But I would like to tell you something about the World of the Elohim, of the Seraphim, and about the central World of rays of the Great Spirit.

Sometimes I was with my Soul Group, sometimes alone. The Worlds you can see on the Cosmic Map were not all the Worlds we saw. We sometimes traveled to foreign planets and visited other star-systems in other galaxies.

Helia was the one who told me about the Elohim. It's quite a

157

short story, because the work of these Masters takes place on so many levels which a terrestrial mind cannot grasp. Their field of activity encompasses our whole Universe.

"First of all I want to talk about the Goddess," she said. "You don't know much about her, even though you were a real lady-killer in several of your lives. I am the Goddess. I carry the energies of the Sun, the Moon, day and night, and all seasons. I'm also the Mother in Everything. I'm yin, Sananda is yang, and if he is the son of God, I'm God's daughter. Together we are Love!

"You men never learned about the Goddess, and that's why males got the advantage on Earth. The position of women has been subordinate. It has not always been like that. It's mostly the fault of the Old Testament that contempt for women has been so conspicuous. In earlier times women were respected all over the Earth. The Mother, the Woman in Confinement, and the mistress were great ideals for more people than you can imagine.

"After that the New Testament came with the woman-hater Paul. It is easy to disdain things that you know so little about! The truth is nowhere to be found, but this is the truth: Sananda and I are brother and sister, born by the same Mother-Father. If this knowledge is written somewhere – and it was on Atlantis – it is destroyed and forgotten. Yet you have the symbol of the yin-yang sphere, where black and white are entwined together in an even, equal eternity. Where is the original meaning of this now? When my brother and I were created, there was no mention of strong and weak. There was absolute equality between strong and weak, where one compensates for the other and where cooperation is not only an image, but action. But the domination of man became a fact, given wings by time.

"The Goddess vanished, but she had to appear again in this century. Male Power is destroying Mother Earth. Some women follow Man in order to enjoy his favors, other women stand powerless as onlookers of the approaching catastrophe. But there are Goddesses, here and on Earth. They cannot appear without some help from women. Bring out the Goddess within you, I beg my sisters. Bring out the Goddess, because she exists deep inside you, even if you don't dare recognize her.

"I have lived many lives on Earth. In one of them I was the Virgin when, as a human, I gave birth to my brother Sananda for the necessary action he was to perform. That's when I became the Mother – before that I was only the sister and the Dual. But I was also Inanna for the Sumerians and Isis for the Egyptians. My last 'performance' on Earth was as Joan of Arc, the brave woman-warrior in France. There I revealed another aspect: the woman as warrior.

"In the beginning there were only seven Elohim, but now there are many of them. They don't work very much with planet Earth, but they take part in the Galactic Council, which is assembled on the Central Sun. The Central Sun has been situated on Sirius A for a long time. Human scientists say that this star is absolutely uninhabitable and consists only of gas fields. Now the reader must accept the fact that when the human eye has cosmic functions and is adapted to new dimensions, the whole 'reality' you believe in changes. Many spiritually active people claim that they have visited the Central Sun. The physical human body would immediately burn there, but if somebody leaves his body to visit other dimensions, he or she may be programmed in different ways.

"Everyone knows about the silver cord, called the dog-leash by Jan. It reaches a long way, but not as far as the Central Sun or Shamballa. It really doesn't reach into the Ethereal World, even if some people say it does. If you investigate near-death experiences you will notice that nobody gets further than the Light or possibly the Akashic Records in No Man's World. People who receive serious messages from the Ethereal World may visit certain domains that are guarded by the Realms of Angels and Masters. If you tear yourself from the silver cord and run away, you must stay on this side. But that seldom happens. When somebody claims to have met the Masters in Shamballa or on the Central Sun they must have got the names wrong for these places. Even I have not experienced the great Secrets."

I have told you many times how vast it is here. I can only tell you my personal experiences after my transition. I can't say definitely or dogmatically this is true. There are endless variations. Again I ask the reader to accept what feels right and true as I go on to talk about the Elohim and the Seraphim.

Elohim are Light-beings beyond our conception. Helia said that they have assembled many highly developed beings and Angels in their Realm. The Angels who have joined the Elohim have chosen voluntarily to work in large groups with the whole cosmos. When I think of the name Elohim I have this vision: "gigantic," "unlimited," "undefinable," and "made of light in different forms." When I asked her if the Realm of the Elohim was like the Ethereal World, she smiled and shook her head.

"Everything is light," she said, "but it is *organized* light. Their World has an unbelievable structure. It is not divided into Realms as here. I cannot describe landscapes or buildings like those that exist here. Yet the Elohim are in contact with the whole Universe, and their galactic network includes contact rays and communication rays too advanced even for us.

"The only beings that are a little more 'real' are the cherubim. You find them there and in the Angelic Realm. The cherubim in the Angelic Realm are a playful group, floating in clouds of love and joy. For the Elohim these same cherubim are messengers, designers, and coordinators. They connect everything that needs connecting, fellowship, and unity. They fly away like glittering breezes, attending to energies and righting wrongs. Errors actually happen up here, too."

I was thinking of all my errors and gave her a nod of assent. On Earth we talk about the human factor. Here we might call it the unexpected factor. You don't expect any mistakes in the Astral World or the ethereal – or by the Elohim. But as long as there are thinking minds there can also be a kind of overheating or flash-over. It doesn't happen often, but it happens.

Let us imagine that the Elohim's World rises over all the others like a giant fountain in a firework display of color and tone. The word "tones" provides a connection to the next World, the World of the Seraphim.

An Opportunity to Ask Master Sananda Questions

"What else but tones can there be close to the Great Spirit, surrounding his radiating World and announcing his Sun World with beautiful sounds?" I asked.

"When we are talking about the Seraphim, we are talking about the Father-Mother at the same time," Sananda answered. "To make it easier for you I'll demonstrate with a metaphor: Imagine a star with many points. The Great Spirit is in the middle and the Seraphim are the points around him. The Seraphim are the outer points of the will of the Great Spirit. They forward his wishes and laws and it always happens through tones, sounds, and music. The tone was the first sound in a quiet and empty Universe. The tone is a creative power, as well as thought. But also the tone must be controlled. The Great Spirit controls the Seraphim and they sing out his message to all of his Worlds."

"I wonder if God or the Great Spirit can show himself in person?" I ventured to ask. "Has he a form or body?"

"Yes," Sananda answered. "He is the Creator. Why would he not be able to create a body for himself, when needed? Who is God? So many people have asked that question. What do you think?"

"If I'm bold," I answered, "I believe God is a very versatile spirit. He must be, in order to be able to survey his creation. I believe that God's eye is in the wind and in all of Nature and in our own hearts. I think he is to be found everywhere where he is loved. I think he laments for those who hate him or who don't want to accept him, and he mourns for those who make war in his name, because he is Love. I think he is the keeper and center of Wholeness. His radiant power is to be found everywhere and in everyone. Then it's up to all of us, both physical and non-physical, to meet his power with our own and say, 'My will is your will!' Only then our soul will shout for joy, because it will gain access to the Divine tones and then we will release our own will, which has kept us imprisoned in its iron grasp."

Sananda gave me a warm smile and took my hand.

"You are so right, Jan," he said. "The Father can take any shape he wants to. He is always with us in the Galactic Council. But he is also the one you describe: a permanent center for Universal Love in the Wholeness. Let's be content with that. We know he is not a stranger who stands high above us; he is one of us when we so wish, and he finds it is right. He accepts our prayers and wishes and he answers when we talk to him, if he thinks we need an answer. He is a rock for the one who gives him total trust. What more can I say?"

"The severe judge and blood-thirsty despot who is called God or Lord in the Old Testament never existed," I thoughtfully answered. "Or did he?"

"Yes, he is a very tangible power from a World I don't want to call good," was the answer, "and his name is Godonda."

"There is one thing I would like to know, Master," I asked. "How can you reveal yourself to people in different places at the same time? Is that also accomplished by the power of thought?"

"In a way, my friend," he answered. "I will be more plain. It is all about projection. I have the gift of projecting myself in different places at the same time. I am here, in the Ethereal World. My projection comes from my aura as kind of a hologram, but not exactly what you call a hologram. If I call it a thinking hologram – how does that sound?"

"It's unthinkable!" I exclaimed. Sananda laughed.

"You see!" he said. "Jan, you are still clinging to many Earthly conceptions. I assure you that the unthinkable can be extremely thinkable and thinking. In fact, it is a talking hologram I send out. Impulses from my brain enter the holograms, which seem to be shapes in compact form, but are completely dissolvable. When I have finished my task, I dissolve the projection with the power of thought. It's a miracle for humans, but for me it is only a technical knowhow. I already knew about it when I was Jesus."

"So at that time you were a hologram?"

"Of course not. I was born to a woman, so I was completely

substantial. But even as a child I had this knowledge in my brain and there was an open channel to my Father-Mother in 'Heaven.' I called it 'Heaven' because it was impossible to explain all the different Worlds in the Cosmos to the superstitious people of that time. Right now you are talking to the core of Sananda. We call the original monad-individual 'the core,' because it's easier for you to understand."

"Then what am I? A spirit?"

"You belong to the Angelic World and you are one of them. You know that. The reality now is as real as when you lived on Earth. But here your life firstly is eternal, secondly it has a much wider perspective, and thirdly you are still 'you.' Your ambition to become one of the Masters means a novitiate of about a thousand years in Earth-time. Are you frightened by this?"

"It may take as many thousand years as it takes," I happily answered. "I'm prepared to be tried again and again. My Soul Group gives me courage and patience every time I meet them – which is often. We are now becoming a team who do not wish to incarnate again. We are closely united and share everything with each other."

"You must know it takes a lot of time before you are ready for a 'thinking hologram,'" Sananda warned. "We are a special group who learned that magic art from our great teacher Melchizedek, the Master over the Masters. His name has been used in many contexts on Earth, but it doesn't matter, because he has many other names. He was a king on Zio when the planet was destroyed by the comet and on Atlantis, long before its fall. He now belongs to the Galactic Council and he is the one of us who totally masters the difficult art of projection. He can be in twenty places at the same time and seem totally physical, but his core being remains in the World of the Elohim."

"Does he belong to the Nine Elders?" I was curious.

"Even if he was, I am not allowed to tell you," Sananda answered cryptically. "Many refer to the Masters as the Hierarchy. We don't like that expression, because we serve the world. We are cosmic servants; we serve the Great Spirit and his closest council, which is very holy."

"That sounds very complicated to me, almost religious," I noticed.

"How do you want it to sound when you are discussing the Creator and his Creation?" asked Sananda, smiling. "Reverence and humility do not yet belong to your virtues, dear friend. Do not protest, I don't want to be critical; it's just a friendly pat on your shoulder. Your curiosity is good, your appetite for discovery even better, and we don't take your disrespect seriously. A fair critical mind gets rid of any exaggeration. But now it's time to send you off on a new adventure! You can't just talk about facts, you have to experience them."

"There is another thing I would like to know before we part," I hurried to say. "What is the truth in all this talk of Ascension to the fifth dimension?"

"The word 'Ascension' is a little deceptive." The one who would really know the answer to my question smiled. "It sounds as if Earth would be shot up into the cosmos like a rocket and all the environment would be transformed into perfect harmony and beauty. People would, as fast as I am waving my hand, suddenly turn into Angelic beings. All violence, all evil, wars, all kinds of ugly death, drugs, gene manipulation, and destruction of the environment – in short, everything that makes money would disappear in a jiffy. Not even I, who was once crucified because of people's lack of belief, believe in something like that. Oh no, to change the world is not that easy. It *will* be changed, of course. The plan is that it shall be transformed, together with its inhabitants, but that change will not be without pain. And please tell me, Jan, what would people learn from such a swift change? Earth is their school, and no school allows its pupils to graduate without an examination. It could not be that easy, because any depth of meaning would be lost."

"The Ascension includes not only the Earth," I objected. "Before that the humans, according to modern 'prophets,' will be migrated in vessels to enormous mother ships where you and others reside. Up there they will choose their destinies or be sent off to another planet, which receives and raises the left-overs."

Sananda laughed loudly. "Now you are exaggerating!" he exclaimed. "It is not decided beforehand where people, including rascals, will be going. It is a completely individual question. I know all about these migrations, which are called resurrections by some. From our side it is a voluntary project. In addition a certain amount of training is necessary, or severe shock may result. I don't deny that migrations have happened and will happen in the future. Also group migrations might happen. But it isn't because of suicide, as some believe, nor mass landings of UFOs that take big crowds of people with them. It happens through silence, prayer, and certain exercises that mitigate the transition.

"Some people have already decided they will be migrated, and they might have wanted it from an early age. We help them because they are already standing with one foot on the other side of the border. But they never come here until they have completed their karma. Many of our sisters and brothers have been sent to Earth with a mission or to finish their own development and, most of all, learn to raise their consciousness in situations where it is needed. They know it is their last incarnation on Earth, and when they come back here they are united with their work-group or Soul Groups."

"Lots of books are written about these migrations – how they will happen, and the exact time for it," I objected again. "As far as I know, no date has been agreed yet."

"Let the Universe keep its secrets. Let the present be the leading power of events. Take care of yourself, dear friend, and don't ponder any more over the future. Let people plan and the Creator reign, or perhaps preferably direct."

A swift hug and the great Master disappeared. I felt a little dazed, sitting in the huge, shimmering Angel Pyramid where I had most of my lessons. It was like a vast puzzle, but some of the pieces were beginning to fit into place, although some were still missing. Would it ever be finished?

17. Alien Contact

The flying saucers had many different names. They were called vimanas, merkabahs, and UFOs. I was taking a trip in one of these when I had an adventure which Sananda had prepared me for.

I have been in all kinds of Worlds. I have visited other planets, sometimes I visited my beloved Mother Earth, and I have fully learned to adapt myself to the life I have here and now. I cannot, under any circumstances, call it "death," because that word means a cold, stiff nothing, placed into the earth or burned on the fire. The inexorable death that people constantly fear doesn't exist. What's the meaning of the peel you put aside when you've eaten the fruit? What do your ragged, old clothes mean when they are ready for the bin? You don't want to use them anymore, and you don't miss them. You are happy to get rid of them and instead wear nice, new lighter garments. There are those in your surroundings who are used to seeing you in your old clothes and can't get over the fact that you have thrown them away. They are really kind of stingy!

I had thought this way already when I lived on Earth and wrote about the old soldier who was so happy when he discovered his new freedom on the church roof with the weathervane. At that time I didn't long for death, but I pondered about what it could mean. I was not afraid of death – as usual, I was just curious. I never had an academic education in that life, but there is something called "education of the heart" and that existed deep in me, because it means truth, justice, and wisdom.

Perhaps that is why I never felt foreign in the Realm of the Angels, even right from the start. Nor in Shamballa. When I lived on Mother Earth people saw me as somewhat strange, especially later on, when I talked openly about an afterlife. I claimed that my life on Earth was

167

a loan and that my real home was "up there." Words like this annoy the learned ones, those who know everything and believe in nothing.

Shala, Zar, and I were sent on a mission. When we sat in the spaceship that took us to Earth, we didn't know its destination. A fourth man had joined us and I didn't know him. He belonged to the "aliens." He had a big head and big eyes, rudimentary features, a thin body of medium height, and only four fingers on each hand. He was a very kind and pleasant man and I liked him at once. He was called Moos. He was the main character in this mission. His body was materialized, because he was going to be a link between us and the Earth. His personality and behavior would be the evidence that aliens are not dangerous and that they would like to co-operate with humans.

Moos was very knowledgeable. He had resources at his disposal which would rescue Earth from being destroyed by its own people. He was prepared to fight with the gentlemen who govern the Earth – not a bad fight, but the challenge from a love-warrior. Just like us, he was invulnerable, but if he was treated badly we had to return. We were supposed to be invisible at his side.

This was a mission concerning high politics. Our spaceship would land in a little place in Canada near a small town where top-level meetings take place. For me this was new and thrilling, especially as I had not followed the current events on Earth since my transition so many years ago. Politics was never my thing, but with the help of Jan, the farm boy, I could achieve enough anger against the benefits and self-sufficiency of those in power. When our ship landed I placed my feet on a foreign patch of earth with the mission to prevent any possible catastrophes.

Frightened people approached the ship. Moos stood in front of it and put his hands up in a warning gesture. People stopped at once. There were three grown-ups and three children. They obviously knew about the danger of radiation from a UFO. Shala, Zar, and I looked closer at the frightened humans. A small girl with brown curls reminded me of someone I loved on Earth, and I sat on my heels and caressed her hair.

"Don't be afraid, little one," I whispered in her ear. "We won't hurt you!"

But the girl neither saw nor heard me. Sometimes it is great to be invisible, sometimes it's a pain. Our plan was that Moos should try to make contact with those people, even if they were suspicious. He talked very good English. He smiled and stretched out his hand towards one of the men. There were two men and a woman. He explained that something was wrong with the ship, and it was being repaired. The older man stood still as Moos came close to him, but he did not shake hands. One of the children, a little boy of about eight, darted forward and gripped Moos' hand. The alien smiled and lifted the boy up. The boy's father asked if Moos would like to visit their home and talk about where he came from and what had happened to the ship. They lived nearby.

Meanwhile, I noticed that the older man took a small device from his pocket and put it to his ear. He talked excitedly into thin air. Later I found out that there now are wireless phones on Earth. Moos sat on the ground and talked in a friendly way with the boy and the brown-haired girl. The mother clutched her baby tightly.

For a while nothing happened. Both men talked to Moos, but suddenly sirens whined and four police cars arrived at top speed. Six policemen emerged from the first one and rudely grasped Moos. He turned to me and winked before two policemen succeeded in pulling a sack over his head. The others ran to the place where the ship had been. It had disappeared. Shala started to laugh out loud.

"Did you see their faces?" she asked me. I was worried about my new friend Moos and I looked despairingly at the vanishing police car. The other policemen talked for a while with the man who had sent for them and after that the grown-ups and the children went with the police. We were standing by our ship, which had become invisible. Hello, reader, this is no science fiction story or an episode of Superman. Ships can be invisible both in the air and on the ground. It's easier for them to dematerialize than for us.

A Political World Conference Gets a Cosmic Visit

"Now it's our turn to move," Zar commanded. We took each other's hands and closed our eyes. Zar muttered something that took us to a large building in the suburb of the small Canadian town. We were invisible now and sat down together on a sofa in a room that looked like a waiting room.

After a couple of minutes Moos arrived and sat down with us. Meanwhile a guard had come and was standing in front of a big double door in the room. Moos pulled up the collar of his coat and pulled down his hat over his forehead. He went to the guard and asked him to open the door. The guard answered that there was a conference going on inside. Then he probably noticed that Moos looked strange and reached for his weapon. Before he could get it, Moos put him in a deep sleep. After that our space man went into the conference room, closely followed by the three of us.

People around the long table were silent and everybody looked at Moos, who had taken off his hat and coat and was standing there in his glittering space suit.

"I greet you!" Moos said in his impeccable English. "I have come here to help you, politicians from many countries, to save Earth."

A man stood up and cried angrily, "Is this some kind of masquerade? Are you the only rascal, or are there more like you? Where is the guard? Get down, everybody, he might have a weapon!"

All the others, about twenty-five of them, hit the floor. It looked funny! I had difficulties not laughing. These fully-grown adults were scared of a small, friendly alien.

"I assure you I am from space," Moos shouted, and showed his hands with the four fingers. "I have come here to help you. I ask to be allowed to take part in this meeting."

"It's a conspiracy!" somebody cried.

"Call the police!" someone else cried.

While the police thought they had Moos in safe keeping, he had calmly left jail. He was standing alive in the conference room and yet no one believed what he said.

"I want to help you by telling you how bad it is on Earth," he went on. "You call yourselves friends of the environment, but you are doing nothing for the environment. You write only empty words. Have you examined the seas after nuclear experiments? Have you taken samples and analyzed the air pollution in the entire world? Do you regularly check the ozone layer and actively eradicate the pollution causing the problems? Can you explain the weather alterations? Have you stopped selling weapons to each other? Have you taken care of the world's drug-trafficking problems, or do you find them a necessary means of extermination? Do you want to eradicate young people? Do you want to allow some of the population in developing countries to starve to death?"

I was so eager to help Moos that I materialized. I heard people talking Swedish in one corner and I thought that perhaps I could tell my compatriots why we were there. I forgot who I was and swiftly changed into the human Jan.

"Look, there's another one!" somebody screamed. "Where did he come from?"

"He forgot to take off his nightshirt!" some witty person cried in the background.

I looked down at myself. I had forgotten to materialize a shirt and a pair of trousers, so there I was in my blue caftan. What was worse: Under it my legs and feet were bare, and my toes were sinking into the soft carpet.

"Does anybody know if there's a carnival in town?" an elderly man asked. "And how did these very odd fellows get in?"

"How do you know it's not the FBI?" cried an anxious female voice. Small black phones were swiftly clamped to many ears, but Moos raised his hand. All the lights went out. He had fused the entire building. I cheered him on silently. Shala whispered to me that I had to dematerialize at once; my voice was not to be heard.

Behind me I heard a quiet chuckle from Zar. He made clear to me in the dark that we are more effective when we are invisible.

Some intelligent people had realized that there were candles on the mantelpiece and they were trying to light them – but in vain. Moos prevented all light, inside and outside. Police cars on their way to capture their escaped prisoner had to stop. They got no further. Those who tried to get into the building met an invisible wall.

We heard agitated voices. Moos called for silence and cried out his message loudly and clearly.

"I am not in fancy dress!" he announced. "I am Moos, a visitor from another planet in this galaxy. We watch in fear as the Earth destroys not only itself, but wreaks destruction far into space and strikes at innocent life there. Invisible workers from a space fleet are working day and night trying to limit all the contamination and poisoning. I was sent here to inform you of this and ask Earth to answer our appeal. There is still a possibility for you to survive and repair at least some of the damages. We want to co-operate. We want to eliminate all the evil happening on your Earth: all the destruction and gene-manipulation that you believe gives you a lead in the Universe. But you now exist at a much more basic stage in comparison with most other inhabited planets.

"When the light returns, none of us strangers will be here. You, who are sitting at this table, have power and influence in your countries. You are making plans in this building for the economic and strategic world-situation. The building is strictly guarded, but you can see that I only put my hand up in order to change it. Devote yourself to the inherited culture you should all take care of. Give your old cultures the chance to recreate the future in tune with the new. If you want to co-operate with us, our knowledge and our practical help is at your disposal – not by force or imprisonment, as is happening to certain visitors. Let your Love meet ours! Realize that Earth has never done you any harm. You are the ones who hurt her. She has shared her abundance with you. You have used it to obtain power in your respective countries.

"I am sorry that I have to talk to you in the dark, but the light did not benefit my message. When you have evaluated the benefits that can be attained by co-operation, you need only zoom in on my name, Moos."

By the time the electricity returned, we were in our space ship. When the police reached the conference building, nothing had happened except that the light had gone out and the politicians were irritated. Later on, we heard that the conference members decided not to take any notice of the alien interlude and did not let the media know about it. I think they thought we were jokers in fancy dress. The truth and the seriousness in Moos' words may have reached the consciousness of some members, but the result was uncertain.

It is a serious state of affairs when people are unable to believe what they themselves have seen and heard. The politicians did not dare believe it. They could not believe a visit from another planet, that there is help for Earth beyond physical limitations, that they can call on Moos for help. They dare not do anything but live in their physical reality. If just one of them could show some compassion or realize the dangers around the corner and discuss them, perhaps a new kind of thinking could begin. But fear and power are bound together, bound by major finance, which brings everything to a standstill. There is no place for alien thoughts. They don't understand that they won't get help until they ask for it.

We had helped Moos with the power outage and with the invisible wall outside the conference building. It was the first time I had taken part in such a major common thought-process and it was good to know how strong we were together without our physical bodies. But it was not the last time we did something like this. Dear readers, what you call the future is full of attempts to bring humans new and positive insights.

174

18. About the Aura and the Chakras

On one occasion when I visited Djwal Khul in Tibet with Zar, I received a very thorough lecture about the aura and our chakras. I believe many of my readers have studied these things, but maybe the little Tibetan has a more unusual teaching method. The adventures of my cosmic life are interspersed with the ancient knowledge from the wise old teachers to make this wisdom easier to understand. In the same way, I intersperse old knowledge with new. Now I will give a brief account of the aura and the chakras for those who don't know about them.

The aura-colors – from the inside to the outside – are red, orange, yellow, green, blue, indigo, and violet. There are of course countless nuances of every color. Red represents the physical, orange the psychic, and yellow the intellect. Those three are strongly connected. The green color stands for Nature, for talents and paths. The two blues and the violet show a rising curve of spirituality.

These seven basic colors are more or less developed in every human being. They can be wholly or partly hidden by diseases and problems, but they exist and they vary, depending upon the different states, capacities, and experiences of the human being. During pregnancy a fan-shaped field is interspersed in the aura of the mother. This signifies the growing embryo, and it leaves the mother at the birth.

The chakras are power centers in the body, consisting of energy formations. The word "chakra" is Sanskrit and means wheel. We see these accumulators of energy as turning wheels, radiating different colors, which have a direct connection to the aura. There are seven well-known chakras:

The Root chakra is red and is to be found at the end of the spine. It guides the physical and the creative parts of man.

The Spleen chakra is orange. It is to be found in the center of the spleen and guides the digestion and the assimilation processes.

The Solar plexus is yellow and guides the adrenal glands, the pancreas, and the liver.

The Heart chakra is green. It guides the heart and the circulation of the blood.

The Throat or Neck chakra is blue. It is to be found back in the neck and guides the breathing, throat diseases, and the thyroid gland.

The Front chakra, or the Third Eye, is indigo-colored. It guides the pineal gland and controls in many ways the psychic mind.

The Crown chakra is violet. It is strongly connected to the Cosmic World.

You may know all this already. If not, it is worth closer examination. The Tibetan has his own version about the co-operation between the aura and the chakras.

When I was sitting with Djwal Khul and Zar in the pretty little house in Tibet listening to his wise words, flowing at the same calm speed as the water in the little lake outside, I was struck by the simplicity of his teaching. The clear sentences were not wrapped in too many words or adornments. They went straight for the spiritual meaning. People make unnecessary difficulties. If a wise man speaks, there is another one who wants to be wiser and add his own ideas to the first wisdom, and the result is a building so high that the foundations cannot support it and everything collapses. This has happened to much wisdom.

"You know about the aura," the Tibetan said, "and you know about the chakras. Many a man has pondered over how to bind these two parts of knowledge to the right system. I will tell you that there is no system. All the chakras have direct contact with the aura, and the radiation between them is automatic when the person is healthy. If there is the least disturbance in the aura or in a chakra, it will make a big difference. I will tell you how and why.

"A chakra is a spinning wheel. Not only that: Every chakra has its colors, connected in a pattern of various fields, like the circles on the Cosmic Map. The root chakra has the least number of fields and the crown chakra has the most. The fields rotate and reveal lots of colors.

176

The colors flow into each other, yet you can see that the lowest chakras have darker nuances than the highest ones.

"If we take the colors I gave you from the start – and they were there from the beginning, even though many people have tried to change them – the colors make different patterns in the wheels. Every color corresponds to the same color in the aura. When considering disease, you must remember that the radiation between chakra and aura must be made in corresponding colors. A chakra is not only a color ball, it contains very strong streams of energy. It is, simply put, charged with energy. When a color from the chakra meets a color in the aura, a certain amount of quantum energy is supplied.

"This charged energy is compressed. Imagine that, by mistake, two colors that do not fit together are brought together. The result may be catastrophic. Because of this, it is important to know if the disease is physical in origin or psychological or mental.

"When you are in good health the chakras rotate swiftly, but if you are sick they rotate slowly or stop. When you need to radiate energy, you must stop the chakra in question. It should not stand still longer than the time it takes for you to loosen an energy ray in the right color and put it in the right place in the aura (with much concentration of thought!). We all have this energy stored up in our chakras, whether we are sick or not, and because of that it is always possible to cure. The energy store is not sick. You can see the chakras as engines of your body, engines that increase or reduce the vibratory rate in your body.

"How do you cure with energy rays of the right color? First you need to know which disease is cured with which color (see page 199). Then you locate the chakra nearest the illness. Then you investigate to see if this chakra is well balanced, i.e., rotating as it should. You cannot use it unless it turns. The cure involves co-operation between the chakra, the aura, and your thoughts, and you start with the chakra. While it is turning, you pull out a spiral from it. The tip of the spiral must find the shortest way to the part of the aura that you are treating. You have to concentrate all the time, your thoughts leading and following what is happening. When the tip of the spiral has reached its target in the aura and your thoughts are concentrated on the idea of curing the illness, the patient feels warmth in that place.

"If there is no feeling of intense warmth, the spiral has not reached its target. Then you have to do it again, making sure that the chakra is moving. (If it is a psychological disorder, your whole head becomes warm, but mostly your crown.) It is not difficult, but intense concentration is needed.

"All people have energy stored, even if they are not interested in alternative healing. This storage of energy is compressed inside the chakra wheel, and that's why you must be very careful when you pull out the spiral. This spiral contains energy that is released as radiation. The whole spiral is applied to the aura to be absorbed there when the radiation is complete. You must extract a spiral every time you radiate somebody. Please note: The radiation is as strong as radioactive radiation, but it is totally harmless because the power collected in the chakra is pure, and out of this power or energy comes an equally pure radiation."

"Imagine," I exclaimed with admiration, "that we all have small storage rooms of pure power in our chakras, without understanding how to use them! If I had known anything about this in my life as Jan, it would have started an avalanche!"

"The time was not right for it then," the Tibetan answered mildly. "An avalanche is needed now. The best result from a chakra treatment comes when you work with love, and for love, with no money involved. I'm sorry to say that the day human beings realize that is still a long way off. Time is money, and it is getting worse. When will human beings learn to live by the laws of Love?"

"Not as long as the politicians are in power," I answered angrily. "I think most politicians choose their profession in order to get rich. I got that feeling in Canada."

"But they really liked your bare feet," Zar teased me. "Maybe it is time for us to appear physically on the arena. There's no point in lamenting over politicians, priests, silly laws, and orders. We must act.

We can send warnings in books like this one, but if the warnings are not heeded, the Galactic Council must act."

"We were discussing the chakras and the aura," I cautiously reminded him. "Have you told me what I need to know?"

"Yes, I think so," the Tibetan replied. "What has been forgotten in this context is the connection of the holy trinity. I call it the Triple Alliance: the aura, the chakras, and thinking in symbiosis. There are many good chakra exercises, but the important thing is that the chakras are spinning. Anybody with sensitive fingertips can do it. You use your whole hand for the four lower chakras. The three upper ones are easy to feel with your index or middle finger. You will feel your fingertips vibrate, sometimes your whole hand if the chakra works right."

"Can it ever spin backwards?" I asked. I was interested.

The Tibetan smiled. "Yours probably is right now," he joked. "Yes, my friend, it can spin backwards. But that's not a good thing, and must be remedied immediately. You have to concentrate on visualizing the proper movements and move your hand or fingers clockwise on the chakra in question. A human being can live with chakras that work backwards, but it will not be a good life."

"I have been reading about the awakening of different chakras," I noted. "Many books on Earth report that our chakras are not awake yet. That means that they do not spin, doesn't it?"

"Oh yes," Djwal Khul answered. "I told you about awakened chakras used with the aura and thought: the Triple Alliance. Sleeping chakras are very common in normal people, those who have no spiritual insights at all."

"Do the chakras awaken by themselves if you have spiritual interests?" I asked.

"In a way," the Tibetan answered. "The chakras are energy suppliers and power distributors in the body, but sometimes they need a kick in order to be conscious of their task."

"We still have our chakras, Jan," Zar commented. "In our ethereal bodies they are power sources that are always in contact with the aura."

"How?"

"They signal to each other!" Zar cried. "They co-operate. We cannot have diseases, because pure thoughts are a requirement in the Ethereal World."

"That would not be possible on Earth," I muttered. "Thank you for an interesting lesson!"

19. About Prayer and Meditation

Prayer is a chapter in itself. I was never very interested in either prayer or meditation. Of course, I have been able to pray at difficult moments, deep inside the dark chambers. When I first came here, this was a problem. I was not used to meditating, but to sitting quietly, pondering. I was very good at that, at least my wife always said so. Meditation is something that has grown up in the last few years, something that started to flower and spread seeds. Its origin is in the Far East, but it was also common among The People of the Sun and the Stars. That's where it started. Transcendental meditation started during my last years on Earth, but I was never interested in navel-gazing. Well, I know it's more than that, and that it involves the word "mantra," which you have to think about. I'm not attracted by that. If I am going to meditate, I want to think about something beautiful, preferably Nature. I can only paint with words, but I always liked good art. I can sit for a long time enjoying a beautiful artwork – isn't that meditation?

When I came here, meditation was the first thing I had to learn in the Angels' School. What an ordeal! Our teachers were patient and humorous, which I needed. I learned to meditate by understanding that it is much easier than you think. If your thoughts are running around like headless chickens you are forgiven. Eventually you learn to close them off and find a kind of vacuum, a blue-white, shimmering fog, where it is easier for you to find the reason or object of your meditation. It didn't involve your navel at all. We meditated on love, friendship, joy, beauty, fellowship, patience, and so on. We could create whatever stories we liked about positive qualities, and afterwards we could ask questions. It was really fun!

The next step was to meditate on Nature. We chose what kind of Nature we wanted to ponder over: flowers, trees, sun, wind, or water

– whatever we thought of. Then we started meditation-journeys, and that is the best thing of all. I still do it as often as I can. Today, I just sit down in peace and quiet and decide where to go – and I go! The journey takes me to many places and situations, always thrilling and instructive. With the help of meditation you can also help others. We often do that in a group. The "broad" Love slowly entered my thinking and my feelings and it is still there, as an intense part of my ethereal person. In this broad Love meditation is always incorporated, with gratitude for everything created and its Creator.

Now we come to prayer. Prayer can be incorporated in meditation, but meditation can also consist of prayer. The power of prayer is very strong. It is of course related to thought, but few people know that whether we say our prayer out loud or whisper it in our hearts, it flies like an arrow direct to the target. Actually it is a combined light- and sound-energy provided with varying vibratory power. When it reaches its target its content is activated in various ways or forms. The prayer is answered. But sometimes the answer is not what you wish for or it may not be regarded as an answer. Why is this so?

Again we come back to the free will of the human being. The will is included in the prayer, and its power varies. You cannot shoot without having a rifle. The will is the rifle. A bullet can ricochet. So can your prayer, if the wrong feeling is behind it. Hatred, envy, egotism, jealousy, greed, love of gain, etc., create the ricochet. A prayer must be offered up with a good intention or as a cry for help. When the prayer is heard, you must give thanks for the help. If you don't and if you move on in an egocentric way, the same problems will return. I believe my readers already know all about this – but do you ever think about it?

The Prayer of Mother Marta

In this context, I will tell you a story that is really a memory from my childhood as Jan.

Old Mother Marta had just become a widow. She was not that old, only sixty-nine. But she was worried and worn-out and she now lived alone in her little red cottage among whispering birch-trees and the fragrance from groves of lilies-of-the-valley. It was early summer and everything was awakening from its winter-sleep, starting to bud and smile at the sun. Dew watered the grass which, pale green and drowsy, rose delightfully from the ground. Up the hill, near the river, where the oaks formed a leafy pillared hall, the yellow anemones glowed in the sun. Mother Marta had neither water nor electricity in her cottage. She read her Bible by the pale light of a paraffin lamp.

She now carried firewood and water alone. When she went to the little outside toilet, one of the holes gaped empty and black. The lid was mostly on, and sometimes the old woman sat there thinking and calmly patting the other lid. She missed her husband Anders terribly, and only wished to die.

Her wish became a prayer. Her widow-pension was not much at that time, but it was enough for her to buy food for herself, the cat, and the other animals. Her husband had left the woodshed full of wood, and her kind neighbor Per helped her chop it when rheumatism ached in her legs.

Marta just wanted to die. Her son had left for America and she had letters from him, but they were difficult to read. She had to ask the vicar for help. She did not like doing so, because the vicar would always tell her how nice it would be for her to move into the old people's home. She did not want to go there at all, she wanted to die in her cottage, like her husband Anders had done. She preferred not to be far from home, for just imagine if Death came and she was not there!

Marta had long conversations with Death. She was hoping that Anders would pay her a visit; she was not afraid of ghosts or phantoms. She thought that maybe she felt him near sometimes, but she couldn't see him. Perhaps he was waiting to appear when he came to fetch her.

Of course she had to take care of the cat and the hens and the pig and the old mare, and she had that very old cow, who gave her such good milk. There was good grazing on the land belonging to the cottage. Her neighbor, Per, who was also old and lonely, helped her with the animals. But her daughter, who lived in the South of Sweden, married to a bank manager, seldom contacted her. She was probably ashamed of her old parents. She sometimes wrote and complained about the old cottage that her husband had inherited.

'How can you complain about an old cottage?' Mother Marta thought. Her cottage was her dearest property, now that Anders was buried under the soil.

It was a bit of a walk to the cemetery, but she went there every Sunday after the sermon. She did not care for coffee after church; the villagers were only curious about how she could manage without Anders. They wanted to make her grief a village matter, which would end in the old people's home. But Marta was not alone. Old Per often came to visit her and have a cup of coffee, and she also had all the animals.

Mother Marta asked and asked to die.

"As soon as possible," she told the Lord. "Then Per can take care of the animals until my children come and ask for their inheritance. I have written a will. You see, my Lord, I don't wish my daughter ill, but she already has everything she needs. My son can have the cottage if he likes. Everything else will go to Per. I am totally finished with this life, you see. I want to go to Heaven, to my Anders, and I want to go now!"

Her prayer rose again and again to the beams in the roof of the cottage. It pierced the timber and turf, and went right out into the cool dusk of the Spring evening. Veils of fog enclosed the meadows in a sweet dampness, and the old cow was mooing out there in the shed. She wanted to be milked. But the prayer danced up into the sky that hung dark and heavy over the treetops, and it carried a melody like church-bells far away, ringing clearly through the thin air.

This time the prayer reached its target. It was caught by a group of merry Angels, who carried it further on towards its target. But the Angels were busy. They were to dance on the Heavenly meadow and play lutes and harps in the Heavenly hall. They planned to sprinkle happy Spring-thoughts on the ground where young couples walked. They had to look after the birds, make sure that they flew to the right places, and care for all the new little animals that were born in the woods. They flew up and down between Heaven and Earth, and all the time they carried Mother Marta's prayer on their wings. In the end it only just managed to cling on!

Mother Marta went to the cowshed and milked her cow. The cat got a saucer of the milk, and then she cooked a pot of rice pudding for herself. Anders had loved rice pudding and she thought that now, as she was going to leave this life on Earth, she might as well eat something really nice, so that she would leave with her stomach full. She was sure that Anders was sitting with the Angels right now, eating the whitest of all rice puddings. What if he was having such a nice time that he had forgotten his old wife?

But Death didn't come. She complained to Per, when he visited. Just imagine, her prayer hadn't helped! Was she so old that the people high up in Heaven didn't care about her? Would Per like to taste her last rice-pudding?

Per smiled, patted her cheek, and called her a silly old lady. You can't ask for Death, can you? Our Lord takes what He wants when *He* wants, not when *we* want. She must have patience, and while she was waiting, she must take care of her little farm. Marta realized he was right. With a sigh, she watched him devour the rest of the pudding.

The beautiful Spring evening was followed by beautiful early Summer and beautiful high Summer evenings. It was harvest time, and Per cut the grass of the meadow outside Marta's cottage in order to have Winter food for the animals. Marta churned butter and made cheese and washed her linen in the brook, enjoying the clear sun of God. Perhaps her prayer for death was weakening these days. Per had a bull, and the bull had visited her cow, and even though she never would have thought it, there was going to be a calf in the cowshed before long. The cat had also been out on an illicit errand. One day Mother Marta's kitchen was full of kittens.

"Do you want me to kill them?" Per asked very carefully.

"Oh no," answered the old lady. "If I am not allowed to die, they won't have that pleasure either. I can keep one or two and give the others away."

Meanwhile something was happening in Heaven. The merry Angels, who carried Mother Marta's prayer on their wings, had a message for a higher Court. There they were reprimanded for not delivering the prayer, but the reprimand was accompanied by a warm smile. It had not been time for Mother Marta, and it was still not time.

Two years had passed since Anders' death. The longing for death by Mother Marta had retreated, perhaps because she was needed by so many. She had her hands full every day, because old Per had cut his leg with the axe in her woodbin. It's fortunate that he didn't die, the old lady thought, and was frightened at her thoughts. Our Lord saved Per for me, she thought, because without him I would be at my wits' end. I haven't got time to die just now.

Instead she asked to be forgiven, for being delayed for her meeting with Anders, up there in Heaven. She really wanted to be there and she longed for her husband, but now she was needed both at home and in Per's cottage. She had worked all her life, so it presented no problem helping her crippled neighbor. In this way, her prayer turned around and became a polite request, if perhaps she could live a little longer to play her part?

Per recovered. Then he wanted to marry Marta. He thought they would get on together. The old lady was terrified. That was something Anders would never forgive. No, it must stay the way it was, even if the villagers gossiped and the vicar called both of them sinners.

It was ten years before Marta died. Meanwhile her hands were full of work in both cottages and cowsheds. If anybody mentioned the old people's home, she became really abusive. She had almost forgotten her death-thoughts and her urgent prayers. Nowadays she loved life! She had not transferred her love to Per, even if they liked each other very much – but she had transferred her love to Life.

It was a gloomy day in September, when the leaves were laying red and golden on the ground outside the cottage. It had been a wearisome day, especially as Mother Marta felt uneasy, and aching everywhere. When Per returned home to his cottage with his stomach full of creamed parsley and perch that he had caught, she felt tired and she lay down

186

on her bed before starting the washing up. While she was lying there with her eyes closed, she suddenly looked up and there was Anders! He smiled and reached out his hands to her, surrounded by a strange light.

'I forgot to wish for death,' she thought, while the light around her husband faded into the light of the dawn in the cottage.

"I'm so tired," she told Anders out loud, because she felt him close to her. "I'm so tired that I would rather like to die."

The small Angels that were flying around her gathered speed in their wings. There was the wish from the old lady again, and this time it would be properly fulfilled. In a twinkling of an eye they went to our Lord. Now he was contentedly nodding, and at once fulfilled the Marta-prayer which they had brought.

That is how the prayer of Mother Marta was at last fulfilled on that Autumn day in the dawn-light, when she fell asleep forever. I, Jan, knew her. She made the best cheese in the world. But this story was about the prayer. It is a story about how a prayer can follow you for many years and you don't believe that our Lord has heard it. One day you ask again from the depths of your heart, and then it is fulfilled, if the time is right. Everything happens when it is *meant* to happen, but not always when *we* want it to happen!

The Creative Power of Thoughts

We are our thoughts! When it comes to meditation, you have to free yourself from thought. When it comes to prayer, you need to keep an eye on your thoughts, to guide them, to feel that they are pure and strong, and give them effusion and power.

When I asked Zar how I could keep my thoughts straight, he answered, "You have to enter the garden of thought. That is where you learn the difference between positive and negative thoughts. The important thing is not to give bad thoughts any strength. If you become absorbed in your thoughts, you give them power, whichever kind they are. There you have the danger with the mass-media. They influence thoughts which have not been called into question. Many people are of the opinion that positive thinking is a fashion cliché. Thoughts are creative. We are not aware that we can create negative thoughts which last and embed themselves in our sub-conscious, only to suddenly pop up like a genie in a bottle when we least need them. This can be destructive."

"How can you convince people of that?" I asked.

"The hard way, I'm sorry to say," Shala answered. "Bad experiences, coming one after another, have a reason. They are caused by negative thoughts becoming action. But you can practice positive thinking. I don't mean you must be positive all the time. Do you understand?"

I shook my head. I was thinking of kind old Mother Marta and her prayers. If you are feeling negative, you can always ask for help. If people knew how many invisible Angels there are around them in the air, in the room, in Nature, they would perhaps feel ashamed and protect their thoughts more. It's all right to ask the Angels for help; that's what they are there for. They always listen, and they must carry the prayer further if necessary. If you are impatient you must wait longer for fulfillment. There is something called karma too, the law of cause and effect. Many threads are needed for a tight weave.

"If you can pray, you can meditate," Zar usually says. "If you can't do either of those, just go on being. In the end, wisdom comes to you, on the day you are standing on the threshold to the unknown, if not earlier!"

20. Who Am I? An Existential Question

Who am I? Why am I me? Will I always be me? What happens afterwards?

These questions have followed me the whole of my life as Jan, and all other lives before that. They have sung in the air, whistled in the trees, rippled in the waves on the lake. They have been a dull whispering in my ears, always and everywhere. They built the foundations of my books, they have danced hand in hand through the thoughts of Jan the poet.

Much is hidden from my eyes still, yet so much has been revealed so that I feel dazed, proud, and humble, all at once. I fight here too, but it is the fight of the spiritual warrior and it is holy and loving – not glorious. Yet I have much to learn, and I enjoy every moment of wisdom and insight that I am still capable of reproducing as words – words to those who will listen, words to those who are wondering. In times gone by, words were only words. Now they are pearls which are part of the jewelry I present to those who want to read my words.

But who *am* I? My dear friend Kualli opened the first sluice gate. We had been out together on a mission and were sitting talking in his garden. I suddenly cried out very loudly, "Who am I?"

"That is your question, but also your answer," Kualli said seriously. "If you haven't got that answer yet, you will have to examine your inner Self. Why haven't you got an answer?"

"Perhaps I'm afraid to know who I really am," I answered thoughtfully. "Maybe all people are afraid of that. But I've been here for so long now and so many wonderful things have happened that I ought to know. Why do I still feel such an uncertainty?"

"We, the Native Indians, used to put the same question to ourselves sometimes," Kualli answered. "But we have an obvious answer: We are the children of the Great Spirit. We are born in Love and we are going back to Love. We are the seed that has grown to a flower and we are the flower that will give seed again. We are the cyclic motion in Nature and the eyes of the Great Spirit."

"How beautiful that sounds," I said. "But it doesn't tell me who I am. I know my origin – but after that? Who am I *now?*"

"The seed was in the origin," Kualli answered patiently, "but it developed into what you are, here and now. Here is always now. Does that help you understand who you are?"

"I circle between Angels' and Masters' Realms, and I am a spirit. My beingness is eternal and everlasting. I am unique. How can I be an unique individual and at the same time have an ethereal body? I have witnessed the little spark that was sailing in space and was turned into a physical person by the Great Spirit. Was I me then or later? I ask you again: Who *am* I?"

"You are who you want to be," Kualli answered firmly. "If you stop wondering who you are, and accept instead that you *are* right now, you solve the problem. You can give yourself innumerable epithets and you can be them all at the same time. Good, happy, warm, cold, friendly, wise, etc. You can be one of them or all of them simultaneously. Then you are *you*. You bring the experiences from all your lives as a little rucksack full of energy on your back. They have all contributed to the growing seed. They are yours, they belong to nobody else. You are the sum of all you have been: from the sparkle in space up to the present. Is that so difficult to understand?"

"Hm," I mumbled, pondering. "Perhaps you are right. Yes, I don't believe I can contradict you. But that begs the next important and difficult question: Why am I *me?* Why am I not you or somebody else? Why did *I* have those experiences in *my* life?"

"Silly question," Kualli snorted. "Why would you be the sum of somebody else's experiences? Everyone is himself and is in himself. Every soul created by the Great Spirit had its pattern from the beginning. When the souls multiplied, right from the start it was wisely organized, so that the patterns were not copied, but were individually characterized. People have very different vibrations, and form a special vibratory pattern. This pattern resembles a subtle and refined aura which is perpetual and follows the human from life to life. We use to call it 'the ethereal original life-pattern.'"

"How does it look for babies?" I asked. "They hardly have an aura, so they can't have an imprinted life pattern, can they?"

"Of course they have!" Kualli smiled. "The life-pattern is embedded into the soul, and even if a baby does not have a full-fledged aura, it is also there. The original colors are there, even if they are weak, and also various gifts. The moment when the soul enters the child differs a lot from individual to individual. When it does, the life-pattern around the aura is characterized."

"Could it possibly be drawn in some way?" I wondered.

"You mean the same way as for instance the priest Edward Warner drew and painted the chakras? His paintings are the prototype for the images of chakras we can see today. But it is not that easy to draw the life-pattern. It vibrates and sends vibrations. It is also a part of the Higher Self and is therefore in a protected zone. You wonder why you are you. It is because you alone have your ethereal original life-pattern. It is a pattern that declares that you are you. That's the answer to both your questions."

"But I have another one," I swiftly remarked. "Will I always remain *me* wherever I go, even on another planet?"

"That question is part of the other ones, my friend," Kualli answered. "The original life-pattern remains for eternity. You cannot end eternity. You can be merged with the light of the Great Eternal Spirit – but not even that makes you lose your identity. Your original pattern has a memory. It can be turned off, but not obliterated. If you live in one place and move to another one, you are the same person, are you not? Don't confuse the external with the internal. In your original pattern there is a life-spark that is called *the monad* by some and *the seed* by others. It can never be lost, and that makes you *you* for all eternity. Are you happy now?"

"Okay," I answered hesitantly. "I suppose I can't get a better answer. I almost understand, you see. But what happens afterwards?"

Now Kualli roared with laughter. "You're quite impossible, boy," he snorted, "quite impossible! There is no afterwards. There is only now."

"I need to plan ahead," I protested.

"The Great Spirit and the Galactic Council do the planning. What is called 'nirvana' in Hindu and Buddhist philosophy is really the merging of the soul into the All – into the Now – into Eternity, parallel expressions for the final Light-experience that people believe is obliteration and total fusion with – yes, with what?"

"The All?" I suggested. "Or maybe God?"

"Or the transition to a Parallel World," Kualli sighed. "There is no total nothingness for the Indians. Our immortal soul is active in many Worlds and never ceases developing."

"Is it possible to develop as much as you like?" I asked.

"Can divine creation be destroyed by any process at all?" was his question. "If nirvana is the total nothingness, there is no longer any logical axiom for the existence of a Creator, because if the Great Spirit exists deep inside our Cosmic Map, he wouldn't be involved with the destruction of souls. Jan, nothing is final. What you call afterwards is actively happening on a higher level. Afterwards is Power, Love, Wisdom, three words that belong together."

"Thank you, Kualli, at last I understand!" I cried, and hugged him. In this way my most difficult questions were answered.

Today, which is Now and which contains all time and no time, I work and study in the Ethereal World. My Soul Group is always present and we learn together. Afterwards we discuss and sometimes question what we learned. We have a very good time together, but we worry for our beloved Mother Earth. Some of us are still working there and they don't send us good news. We want to see Earth blossoming in all her beauty, growing into a happy, jolly, lovely planet.

I have dictated this book for the ordinary human being who is trying to protect Earth as well as he or she can. I want to open your eyes to life on the other side of death, but I also want to tell you about all the help that is around you at times when the Earth is in real danger. Those who rule the world only think of power and profit, and they do not care about the common people. They are sacrificed in many ways. They are afraid. They do not dare disturb the guardians of power. War, violence, and disease are spreading across the beautiful surface of the Earth. No one dares suffocate the evil.

You, who want to contact us, can do that through prayer and

meditation. We have no right to go against your free will, and as long as you don't object, we must believe that your free will rules the world. We will not persuade you to think otherwise. It must come from yourselves. We have talked a lot about the power of thought in this book: how thought is able to create both positive and negative. That is no exaggeration, no fantasy. Try, and you will see! But you will have to concentrate or nothing will happen.

I, Jan, have told you what has happened to me from the beginning of time, when I was only a small dot of cosmic energy. I don't expect you to believe me. Maybe somebody else has written about life on the other side in a way you prefer. You should know that I am writing in *my* own words with *my* own perception. Another writer may tell of other things because the spirit, giving him inspiration, has had other experiences and describes them in other words. Kualli says, "My reality is not yours," it is *unique* and *individual.* I need to point out that you should listen to your inner voice, your intuition, the voice that gives you warnings and advice from deep within your Self.

Remember that life is not only the one you live on Earth now! Life is to a higher degree the one you meet on the other side of the Golden Portal. If there was no mass-media you would perhaps not believe that there are countries on Earth with exotic fruits, hula-hula-dance, and cultures far removed from your own. Not until you went there would you discover other ways of living and other customs than the ones you know about. You love your body and you don't want to lose it, do you? But it is only the withered, worn-out body that you lose when you die. Everything else is still there. You will get a nice new body, you will feel young and vigorous, and you can think and feel as much as before – no, in fact even more! You will not fly around here on Angels' wings, tooting on a trumpet. We work here, but we work with things that we enjoy doing. Furthermore, you get help and appreciation. You need not miss anything, least of all money. So, why are you afraid of death?

Not one single day since I came here have I missed night. Not for a moment have I wanted to return. You can have the dubious joy of returning to Earth to reincarnate – if you like. But you can also work with your near and dear ones from here, provided you don't control them, or interfere in their will. Here there are possibilities at your disposal that you wouldn't even dream of!

You call Earth a school. It is a difficult and problematic school, with good and bad classes. Sometimes there are so many pupils that there are not enough classrooms. Then the pupils must wander around. They get diseases and they starve. It seems that this school is unjust, but the Great Spirit is never unjust. He is Love. People forget that when they suffer, but they suffer in order to learn. They themselves have chosen to go down to Earth and suffer. Each of you has, yourself, chosen your time, your surroundings, your talents and your karma. If you give up, you have to do it again. But just as you can create a miserable life, you can create a good life. It depends on you yourself, on your thoughts. So hurry up now and guide your thoughts the right way: to joy, love, friendship, success, fellowship … and much more.

I won't say farewell, but "Au revoir!" which you must interpret as you will. Maybe I will write another book or I will stand here in the gateway, waving my hand when you pass the border. I don't worry about the future, because it doesn't exist. The future is the same as "the Emperor's new clothes." The Now is eternal and wonderful. Every second is a flower, a ray of joy and hope. Imagine! Every day is a new miracle. See the Sun, even if the sky is gray. The Sun is behind the gray clouds as sure as you are standing there watching.

You are standing on an Earth that radiates with the glittering light of the stars. You are looking at stars that are mirrors of your own inner light. You are the extended arm of the Great Spirit on Earth. You are the one who rakes your path, cultivates your soil, and cares for your sick mother. Your gift to Earth is *you, yourself.* You are a part of it, and that's why you must feel well. You feel well when you want to be happy and glad – you want that, don't you? Otherwise the Sun disappears behind the clouds and the stars grow dim with your grief. You must know this: Earth doesn't belong to the human being. The human being belongs to Mother Earth.

Dear human being, you carry a proud and gleaming secret: You are descended in a direct line from The People of the Sun and the Stars!

Appendix

The Cosmic Map – Explanation and Guidance

The Cosmic Map on page 3 has a starry sky as its background. The planets of our galaxy can be found there, as well as some constellations.

The outer ring (1) on the map is called *"Universal Worlds."* It contains several Realms, but we have chosen to name only two of them: the Realms of Darkness and the Realms of Idols. The idols that have existed from ancient times, worshiped under many names by people, have their own Worlds. It means that they still exist in their own surroundings without any contact with humans. We don't know very much about them except that their names are to be found in history books. These books do not reveal that these idols weren't human imagination, but that they really existed and acted as powers or energies in the human world throughout time. Some of the idols were created by human thoughts. These idols still exist in the Realms of Idols like shadows in eternity. The others, the strong, the well-known, those who even today have their worshipers, are still alive and working.

We prefer not to talk about the Realms of Darkness. We have enough of their powers on Earth. They are the Realms that Lucifer first created in his wrath against the Great Spirit – something he bitterly repents. They grew to such an extent that he could no longer control them. But they are still there and their Realms must be noted.

The next circle (2) contains the *No Man's World.* It is the transition Realm for souls where everyone comes after death, whether they just pass or stay for a while. As you see, there are tunnels from Earth directly to No Man's World. This is where souls wander around until they find their goal. They are never alone. They have help from millions of Angels.

If they want to continue, they are immediately carried further on. The confused ones who refuse to believe they are dead must stay there until they, themselves, wish to go on.

What is called hell and purgatory in the Bible is included in the gigantic space of No Man's World. These states exist in various forms which are all based on the fact that the souls live in the surroundings they have created until they awaken to the possibility of further development. Souls who on Earth were infiltrated with money transactions have to continue forever with such things until, one day, they discover the emptiness and senselessness of what they are doing. Criminals can continue with their crimes in a one-sided way until they get tired of it and want to change their situation. Murderers experience darkness until they cry for light. In contrast to the menacing prophesies of the Bible, these servants of darkness are often confronted with Angels of light. We really respect those Angels who have taken on the difficult task of changing the ones who hang on grimly to their old bad selves. They all get the chance to return to the light. Nobody is too bad to deserve help and positive changes.

People who neither believe nor disbelieve and during their lifetime seldom give themselves a chance to think about the secret of Life – what happens to them? It varies, depending on their unique minds and voluminous egos. Usually they are put in situations that make them react and start to consider. There are helpful Angels at hand. Forgiveness is always nearer than you think!

After that we arrive in the *Astral World* (3). So much has been mentioned about that World in this book that more explanations are not necessary. Here there are health care, schools, science and research, animals, children, dreams, art and music, and the Akashic Records, which recount the development of every human being during all their lives. The hospitals take care of people who don't understand that they were free from their illness when they died. Many cannot accept this. Some souls need mental help.

The *Nature World* (4) is near to the Astral World. All kinds of Nature Spirits live there, and it watches over Nature on Earth. Among the Nature Spirits are what you call fairy tale spirits, who lived quite physically thousands of years ago and who still remain in fairy tales and narratives of most ancient cultures. Here there are goblins, elves, giants, trolls and fairies, the Neck, the wood-nymph, mermaids, and other little people.

People nowadays who have seen brownies cannot doubt the reality of fairy tales. There are also trustworthy people who have seen elves, giants, and trolls in the Northern forests. The author has met many of them.

One step further towards the middle of the map there are *Parallel Worlds* and *Incarnation Worlds* (5). We will not describe these Worlds here, because there are too many and they are too complicated to be explained in any simple way. They are parallel to each other and have at the same time many dimensions. They are tied together in a pattern, not visible to human eyes.

The *Ethereal World* (6) that is next is described very well in the book. It contains only two Realms: the Angelic Realm and the Realm of the Masters, which are gigantic conclaves in the enormous musical work created by the Great Spirit. These Realms are ruled by beauty, love, and wisdom, and the human who transfers directly from death to these Realms is a very lucky person.

Something else we find difficult to understand is the *World of the Elohim* (7). We only know that the Elohim work across the whole galaxy and that they are involved in the Galactic Council.

The *World of the Seraphim* (8) is nearest to *the Great Spirit* (the center). Seraphim are a kind of Angel. The Seraphim are masters of music. Their wonderful music surrounds the highest Deity in our galaxy. The Seraphim move rhythmically in a cosmic dance that is not what we would call dance. They sing, but so do Angels. Song and music are an everyday part of life in those high spheres.

The Light that emanates from the inner Deity, the Great Spirit, is a light of Love, and it also contains the Tone, the original tone which created for the Creator. The inner core needs no explanation, *it is*.

The Cosmic Map does not claim to be the true one. Every cosmic idea has its own reality and every human being accepts what he or she feels right. The purpose of the Cosmic Map is only to create a simpler image than those shown in the "old books." The map is what I learned in the Angels' School and what I feel is important to show on a physical level. People have their own free will and therefore they have the right to acquire knowledge that they like without being indoctrinated by something they feel is wrong.

The Original Meaning of Colors

There are seven original colors that correspond to the colors of the rainbow. You can use white anywhere, because all colors derive from white.

Red: stimulates blood circulation and increases body temperature. It helps tiredness, shivering, anemia, and colds. Red is stimulating, and therefore a good color to use for depression.

Orange: helps the digestion and is useful for stimulating the processes of distribution and circulation in the body. Good for problems with the spleen. It is used for kidney diseases but also eases bronchitis and other lung diseases. Orange stimulates physical energy and the mental faculties and is used to alleviate inhibition and repression.

Yellow: facilitates digestion and has a cleansing effect on the liver and intestines and cleans the whole system. From a mental health point of view, yellow is as stimulating as sunshine. Yellow eases stress, skin problems, constipation, and liver problems. Yellow is a good color for the diabetic.

Green: has a reconstructive effect. Sick cells may be neutralized and rebuilt with green. Green is good for normalizing blood pressure and helps the heart to work properly. It is also good for headaches and colds.

Blue: stops infectious diseases and has an antiseptic effect. This color brings calm and is good for the nerves. Blue eases throat problems and can be used for all childhood illnesses. It is also good for inflammation, spasms, insect bites, itching, headaches, insomnia, and menstrual pain.

198

Indigo: controls the pineal gland and cleans the blood. It is used for all eye diseases and nose and ear problems. Good for lung diseases and asthma. Indigo is a very good complement to the other colors.

Violet: relaxing and comforting for the nerves. Eases mental problems, rheumatism, tremors, and bladder diseases.

It is also a good idea to consider the color of the food you eat, because it is important for your health and may affect any illness. For instance, if you are nervous, it is good to wear a yellow garment and eat yellow food or fruit, etc.

List of Diseases and Colors

The colors are not a cure in themselves, but they can alleviate pain if they are used alongside suitable natural medicines.

Ache	all shades of blue
Agony	violet, indigo
Allergy	blue, yellow, violet
Anemia	red, orange
Anorexia	blue, violet, orange
Appetite, loss of	red, green
Arteriosclerosis	violet, green, red
Asthma	indigo, blue
Bladder	violet, yellow
Bleeding, external	blue, indigo
Blood circulation	red, orange
Blood pressure, high	green, blue
Blood pressure, low	orange, indigo
Brain diseases	blue, violet
Bronchitis	orange, indigo
Bulimia	blue, violet
Burns	all shades of blue

Cataract	indigo, green
Childhood illnesses	all shades of blue
Cold	blue, red
Colic	blue, indigo
Constipation	yellow
Cramps	blue, violet
Depression	red, orange, violet
Diabetes	yellow
Diarrhea	blue, indigo
Digestion trouble	yellow
Ears	indigo, green
Epilepsy	yellow, blue, violet
Eyes	indigo, blue
Female problems	yellow, blue, indigo
Fever	blue
Fibromyalgia	blue, yellow, orange
Flatulence	blue, violet
Flu	indigo
Foot problems	blue, violet
Gall problems	yellow, blue
Giddiness	orange, blue
Glaucoma	indigo
Goiter	indigo, red
Gout	blue, violet, red
Hands	blue, yellow
Headache	green, blue
Heart problems	green, red
Hemorrhoids	blue, green
Immune system	blue
Insect bites	all shades of blue
Intestines	orange, yellow

Jaundice	blue, green, orange
Kidneys	orange, violet
Liver	yellow
Lumbago	blue, indigo
Lung diseases	orange, red, yellow
Lungs	violet
Menstrual pains	blue, indigo
Mental health	blue, violet
Metabolism trouble	yellow, orange
Muscle pains	green
Nervous system	yellow, blue, violet
Nose	indigo
Nosebleeds	indigo, green
Psoriasis	yellow, orange, indigo
Rheumatic diseases	violet, blue, red
Sciatica	indigo, violet
Sinuses	yellow, green
Skin diseases	yellow
Stomach pains	blue, yellow
Stress	yellow, violet
Throat problems	all blue colors
Toothache	all shades of blue
Tremors	violet
Varicose veins	indigo, blue
Weariness	red, orange
Wounds	green, yellow

Made in the USA
Columbia, SC
03 July 2017